Charlie Nicholas

Charlie Nicholas

The Adventures of Champagne Charlie

David Stubbs

BXTREE

First published in 1997 by Boxtree, an imprint of
Macmillan Publishers Ltd, 25 Eccleston Place, London, SW1W 9NF
and Basingstoke

Associated companies throughout the world

ISBN 0 7522 2466 2

9 8 7 6 5 4 3 2 1

A CIP catalogue record for this book is available
from the British Library

Typeset by SX Composing DTP, Rayleigh, Essex
Printed by Mackays of Chatham plc, Chatham, Kent
All photographs © Colorsports

For their invaluable help in putting this book together, I should like to thank the following: John Colquhoun, Danny Crainie, Phil Gordon, George Graham, Nick Hornby, Roy McCormack, Kevin McKenna, James Payne, Graham Rix, Alan Smith and Tom Watt, and all the staff at McNeill's Bar.

Chapter One

April 5 1989. Wembley Stadium. The very first Littlewoods Cup Final. Littlewoods. The Pools people. Even at the height of Thatcherism, the notion of corporate sponsorship seemed sufficiently naff and new to stick in the craw. All those footballers forced to run around in shirts endorsing Crown Dulux Paints, or worse, Danka and Virgin, it was demeaning to grown professional men. Still, Littlewoods was better than the short-lived Milk Cup. Wholesome and full of calcium as milk was, the notion of dairy products in conjunction with competitive sport always seemed to have the unfortunate ring of the egg and spoon race about it.

What we were talking about, in truth, was the League Cup, founded by Alan Hardaker in the early sixties. It had never quite managed to establish the kudos of the Football Association Challenge Cup, with its grand tradition of white horses, the Matthews Final and Ronnie Radford's 35-yard screamer. Its winners were a ragbag, dubious assortment of Norwiches, West

Bromwich Albions, Swindon Towns and so forth, as if the bigger clubs, the 'proper' clubs, had far better things to do than be bothered to exert themselves for such a lowly engagement.

By 1987, however, though, the aristocrats of Liverpool had deigned to show a flash of speed in the competition. They'd been absent from any of the first 20 or so finals – suddenly, they'd won three or four on the trot. And here they were again in 1987, facing up to Arsenal, still a big name even if their recent tally of non-triumphs didn't appear to merit it. The newly-launched *When Saturday Comes* had recently run a sarcastic tribute to the club, bowing low in mock-gestures of awe, 'We gaze with envy at their five post-war trophies.'

Liverpool-Arsenal. They'd met in finals twice before, in 1950 when the mighty Arse had won 2-0, thanks to the splendid contribution of Joe Mercer, and then again in 1971, when Arsenal had pulled off an unlikely, if much-deserved double, with Charlie George, footballer's one-man equivalent of the glam rock era, knocking in the winner before prostrating himself in almost licentious, sexual triumph at the final whistle. Naughty boy.

Now they were meeting again and this time, another naughty Charlie was being mooted in some quarters as the possible star of the show – Charlie Nicholas.

Charlie had come down to Arsenal four years earlier from Celtic, hailed like a sort of Scottish Dick Whittington lured, in tabloid speak by the 'bright lights' of the capital city. While the bright lights of the paparazzi certainly flashed incessantly every time he set foot across the portals of any of London's then-fashionable nightclubs, the tag was a daft, quaint and patronising one – the 'bright lights', with the strange suggestion that folk north of the border had yet to hook up to the national grid and groped about by the dim illumination of oil-lamps outside the hours of daylight.

Still, it had struck and had been sufficient to arise the hackles of new Arsenal manager George Graham. A blazer-and-grey slacks man by individual temperament, he looked askance at the seemingly flamboyant Charlie, trailing his reputation behind him, one of several players at Arsenal who appeared to be on the point of outstaying their contractual welcome. In well over 100 games over the course of four seasons, Charlie Nicholas had scored fewer goals for Arsenal than he had in one astounding season at Celtic which had prompted a feeding frenzy of transfer speculation some four years earlier. Though it had been all strained smiles and photo opportunities on his arriving at Highbury, Graham made several ominous remarks, including one in an early television interview: 'Standards in British society are falling. I'm going to make sure, however, that they don't fall at Arsenal.' Ramrod rigidity, team effort and discipline were to be the new order of the day – flamboyant, wayward, skittish, invidualistic Charlie Nick had been invited to read and digest the writing on the wall.

That said, in spite of yet another inconsistent season, George Graham was looking to his inherited young charge to make the difference on this, the first big day of his Arsenal regime. 'We will be on the look-out at Wembley for Charlie's sense of the big occasion. I think we shall see him rise to his best and give everybody something to think about,' he commented. And fair comment it was. While Charlie might have lacked consistency, seeming to fade enigmatically in and out of form, he almost always produced the rabbit out of the hat when it counted. When back up in Glasgow, against Rangers. When at Arsenal, against Spurs. Gloriously, memorably, the sort of goals travelling troubadours would have composed ballads around in bygone ages. Liverpool themselves had known the waspish edge of his mercurial incisiveness more than once over the past few seasons.

Then again, it might have been a bit of a long-shot, psychological geeing up of an unfulfilled talent they had to make the best of a bad lot of circumstances. Truth was that Arsenal's presence in this final against the magisterial Liverpool was regarded in many quarters as almost an impertinence. Arsenal were one of the Big Four or Five in the First Division but there was a strong sense that they were a small team, compared to Northern giants such as Manchester Utd and Liverpool. Small pitch, small players, small horizons, small-minded tradition. No one could believe it when Charlie Nicholas, the most sought-after talent in the country, had spurned the advances of the Big Two in favour of Terry Neill's struggling North London outfit back in 1983. Against the cultured, long-limbed, aristocratic, footballing success machine that was Liverpool, the wretched Arse were regarded as scurrying little runts, barely worthy to share the same turf as the Red thoroughbreds who would doubtless charge through the Arsenal ranks like an élite Crimean cavalry scattering so many rural peasants. Small matter that Arsenal had, amazingly, headed the First Division in the run-up to Christmas. The natural order had soon restored itself as Liverpool, almost sup-pressing a yawn, had galloped back to lead the field in the final furlongs of the season. Meanwhile Arsenal, true to recent form, had muffed it again, having only won one league game in their last seven and bumbled right back to the place they should have known as theirs to begin with. Certain elements in the tabloids had jeered that Arsenal were only there to make up the numbers, to provide token stooge resistance as Liverpool gathered in yet more silverware. True, Liverpool's form had stumbled once or twice recently and had lost influential defender Mark Lawrenson to injury during a needy encounter at Wimbledon a week earlier which they had lost 2-1. But they were overwhelming favourites.

Oh yes, Arsenal would once again have to endure the cringe, the cringe to their north-western betters. Yet while Liverpool were the natural aristocrats on the pitch, off it the cultural situa-tion was quite the reverse. This was 1987. While London pride was booming with an explosion of barrow boys coining it large in the wake of the big Thatcherite yuppy explosion, Liverpool was the hapless victim of rapacious Tory policies, with the docks decimated and the whole city a pitiful, wasted realisation of Alan Bleasdale's worst nightmares. And did the Arsenal fans have any sympathy? Did they chuff. This had been touted as a 'friendly final', with family enclosures and so forth, evidence of the game's determination to counter its recent hoolie-infested image. But there was nothing very chummy about the way Arsenal fans lined the walkways to Wembley, jeering the arriving Liverpool fans, waving wads of fivers in their faces – a typical North London greeting of northern teams which would inspire

Harry Enfield's 'Loadsamoney' character. It was all par for the course in those jolly days of cockney sneering at northern misery, and jokes such as what do you call a Liverpudlian in a suit? The accused.

Once inside the stadium, however, the arrogant swagger would be all Liverpool's. A glorious red sea of Anfield faithful were in full song, a throng who didn't just revel in the knowledge that theirs was the greatest football team in the land but luxuriated also in the knowledge that they themselves, the fans, were held in special affection by neutrals the world over – the 'greatest set of supporters in the world', 'worth a goal a game'. All of this still held true in spite of the brickbats that had been unfairly hurled their way after Heysel less than two years earlier. Liverpool fans always had an air of the chosen ones.

Arsenal fans were equally red and equally noisy but they knew deep down they weren't held in special affection by neutrals. Forced to admit you were an Arsenal supporter and the temptation was to clear your throat apologetically, Eric-Morecambe-style. It was like admitting you voted Tory at the last election. Arsenal fans were pariahs, potato heads, who, in supporting a team so manifestly unstylish were making a bad fashion statement about themselves, like Skoda drivers or shell-suit wearers. Not the chosen ones. No pedigree. Look at the managers. Liverpool had Dalglish, Paisley, Shankly. We had had Howe, Neill, Mee. Seemingly smaller men. Bill Shankly once said, 'There's only two teams in Liverpool – Liverpool and Liverpool reserves.' Bertie Mee once said – well, no one cared what Bertie Mee ever said. He'd only won the double for Arsenal but somehow, so what?

Same for the players. Liverpool: Hansen, Neal, Rush, Dalglish again. Arsenal: an unhandsome array of Talbots, Sansoms, Mariners, a rag-bag of Ipswich rejects and dodgy moustaches. But then there was Charlie. At least there was Charlie. At a time when stars like Liam Brady and Frank Stapleton had been allowed to slip away, Charlie Nicholas had been drafted down to supply not just goals but a dash of panache, a swish of blade to head up Arsenal's doughty but undistinguished-looking infantry. You could talk about boring boring Arsenal but never boring boring Charlie. A player renowned as much for his hedonistic and occasionally ill-advised adventures off the pitch as well as on, he wasn't going to be awe stricken by Liverpool, Wembley, or the big occasion.

Yet as Charlie and the team clacked their studs out of the dressing room, chewing pensively, trying to shake off the debilitating jelly-layer that seemed to set around their lower limbs as pre-match tension set in, even he, for all his cheek and rowdy banter, must have been a little apprehensive. He knew as much as anyone else that today was make or break day, shape up or ship out, put up or shut up. Tabloidese imperatives would be ringing in his ears. George Graham had never particularly liked the cut of Charlie's jib, nor the twinkle of his earring. That said, he knew that today, in Charlie's first cup final since arriving at Highbury, might be the day Charlie finally, in workman's terms, delivered the goods. Talking to the *Sun* about speculation that he might have to leave Arsenal at the end of the season if he couldn't agree terms, Charlie added wistfully, 'It would be fantastic to score a couple of goals against Liverpool at Wembley on Sunday.'

The rumble became a muffled chanting, the muffled chanting a low, heavy cheer of anticipation, and the cheer of anticipation a blazing, deafening roar as the players finally strode out on to the carpet green turf of Wembley, led out by George Graham, back straight, as if leading a Boys' Brigade to the jamboree. Nice spring day, first final of the season, Brian Moore in the commentary box, curtains drawn, phone off the hook, beers and mates in, all right with the world. On the pitch itself, the opening ceremony, with Sir John Moores, the elderly President of Littlewoods Association lining up with the officials, looking as fragile and doddery as a Young Mr Grace as he met the players – ('You've all done very well!' 'Er – they haven't kicked off yet, sir.'). Or rather, the players met him. In an unusual reversal of protocol, each team member took it in turn to trot up to Sir John and shake hands, wedding-reception style, perhaps out of respect to the inventor of football pools' creaky limbs. Sir John Moores. Another grand old Scouser. It must have been hard for Arsenal not to feel everything was loaded against them.

Still, the Arsenal fans were defiant, their end a vast rally of euphoric red and yellow, banners waving, hastily sewn bedsheet banners screaming 'CHA-CHA-CHARLIE!' fluttering aloft. They were underdogs – they didn't care.

The referee, a Torquay policeman, whistled for kick-off. The chorus subsided, backsides sank back on to seats, a low, tense beehive drone of anticipation. A typically cagey start, tentative parries back and forth in midfield. Only two minutes in and Charlie got the ball – almost a squeal of excitement from the Arsenal end, like when Charlie got the ball. Excitement as he turns Alan Hansen in one, shimmying twist but disappointment as the ball runs away from him.

Early days. Arsenal came forward with impertinent little parries but Liverpool shepherd them away. 6′4″ Niall Quinn manages to connect from a corner set piece but in the big-match cauldron his lanky frame seems to encase the spirit of a small, nervous boy, and he misdirects it completely. A few minutes later, the first real chance as Liverpool finally test their opponents' strength. Ian Rush takes predatory advantage of a lethargic O'Leary on the ball deep in the Arsenal half, slides in, emerges with the ball at his feet and the Irishman left for dead, slips it across the box to Craig Johnson who places it hard and low, with gangly Arsenal keeper Lukic forced to crumple into a prostrate heap just inside his right post to save.

Arsenal are making chances but not making the most of them. A free kick. Davis tees it up for Charlie Nicholas but he pats it ineffectually into the Liverpool wall. Now Liverpool begin to flow forward in ominous formations, gathering pace, bad perms like equine manes flapping in the breeze as they assume their natural authority over the game, a white cavalry (Arsenal won the toss on home kit) scattering the reds. It's like watching third-formers pitted against the prefects' team. A shot from the outrageously fat yet graceful and lethal Jan Molby, Liverpool's Danish midfielder, whistles over the Arsenal bar. A warning shot. When Arsenal try to attack back they are easily subdued by

Whelan and the magisterial Alan Hansen. Rush, meanwhile, is sweeping past the worryingly slow Adams and O'Leary at will.

Then, against play, the ball breaks to Nicholas. Another vocal swell of anticipation as he scampers forward – but it's a bad ball, a hospital ball to Niall Quinn out on the right.

Liverpool are straight back. Molby picks up the ball in deep midfield and in what seems like a thick cluster of shirts picks out in an inkling the one pass that will leave Arsenal dead-footed, unpicking their defence like a dodgy Yale lock. McMahon is through. Arsenal desperately scramble back but Rush has joined him in the penalty box. Two against one. McMahon trickles it across to Rush who slots it past Lukic with an absolutely typical goal. Twenty-one minutes gone. The cheer that greets the goal is like the sort of cheer that would greet the tenth goal in a 10-0 thrashing. Too easy.

Well, that's it, now. Arsenal really might as well turn it in and go home. Ian Rush is Liverpool's talisman. No one needs a John Motson to tell them that when Ian Rush scores, Liverpool never lose. It's never happened. Literally. Not in 100-odd games. He's like Excalibur. So that's that. The only question now is, how many more?

Liverpool are dominant. Alan Hansen is beginning to come upfield, surging through Arsenal like a Beckenbauer through butter. But it's not all one way. Arsenal are hanging in there, under-doggedly. Nicholas gets it out on the right and tries to pass through the bodies of defenders ghost-like. He's done it before so many times in the past – found gaps between bodies that simply didn't exist and spirited his way through into the box. This time, his little jink flounders on a pile of Liverpool bodies and boots. Not today, sonny.

Instead of consolidating, Liverpool seem to be toying with Arsenal, teasing them, waving them in only to brush them off like flies. But Quinn and Nicholas are beginning to cohere, put little moves together. Nothing Liverpool can't handle, but then, from yet another thwarted Arsenal attack, the ball runs loose to Paul Davis and he lofts in a 25-yarder that kisses the right post, just past the outstretched right hand of the dramatically airborne Grobbelaar. Eyebrows raise. Arsenal continue to peck around the edge of the box as balls are floated in. Niall Quinn takes an elbow smack in the face from Alan Hansen. An accident, perhaps but a free kick certainly. McMahon screams at the referee though it's hard to see what about.

They've rehearsed this one. It's almost a Busby Berkeley number. Steve Williams stands astride the ball with Hayes looking to tap it through Williams' legs to Charlie Nicholas, posed on the balls of his feet like an old-school sprinter. Instead, however, he back-heels it to Davis as Nicholas shades off to the right, a decoy. The subsequent chain of events take place over the course of about ten seconds. Davis rifles in a shot – straight into the gonads, unfortunately, of the hapless Niall Quinn, still groggy from that elbow incident. Quinn collapses in agony. Kenny Samson is first to the ball, floating it over the charge of Liverpool defenders to Viv Anderson, who's drifted into the box unnoticed behind Spackman. Anderson pokes it through a crowded box to Adams, whose shot bounces off Gillespie's arm. While both teams react, nervously or indignantly to the possibility of a penalty, Charlie Nicholas still has his eye on the ball. He darts in four yards out with everyone else caught on the back foot and, astonishingly, toe-punts it against the post – aargh!! How did he find the post from there? But Liverpool aren't safe yet. The ball tumbles back out to Anderson who blasts the ball across the six-yard box – where Nicholas, loitering among a pack of bewildered defenders, reacts quickest with a neat, instinctive tap-in from six inches out.

As the Arsenal end, in front of whom this comedy of errors has been played out, writhe with delirium, Tony Adams sprints after Charlie, grabbing him in an elbow lock of sheer joy, almost garrotting him in his moment of glory. 1-1, half an hour gone and Liverpool aren't singing any more. Still, Ian Rush, and all that. Never lost. Not to worry, lads. Technical hitch.

Charlie's bustling with confidence now – he turns a couple of defenders like Charlie Chaplin outwitting a pair of burly stooges and is rewarded with an 'Ole' from laughing fans, revelling in his bounty. But his pass goes nowhere.

A minute or so later, it's all turned bad again. Charlie is limping. It's his ankle. An unspoken 'Not again' rings silently around the Arsenal end. His whole career has been blighted by a series of injuries, from niggly hamstrings to the broken leg he'd suffered as a 20-year-old. How many times have fans watched in dismay as he limped off the field, victim of the attentions of hard-bitten defenders, determined, often under instructions from managers, to 'do' Charlie? The physio's forced to do a 300-metre dash around the stadium to get to Charlie – but it's getting near to the interval and after some heavy strapping, he's able to re-emerge on to the field of play, to cathartic applause, as the half is played out in a spirit of detente, with mutual respect between the teams now established. Even so, some of the younger Arsenal players such as Quinn look a little fazed – and it's Charlie who's geeing up and exhorting his nervy, subdued colleagues as they troop into the tunnel. He knows they can win.

The second half. Rush makes an early breakthrough but the Arsenal back four have got the measure of him – they can't catch him but they can catch him offside and they're beginning to do so regularly. He's getting frustrated. Another chance for Liverpool. The ball bounces off the head of a temporarily disorientated O'Leary in midfield and falls to the feet of the stampeding Spackman who's all but clean through. O'Leary, naughty boy, gets back and chops him down from behind. Outside the box but fair does, a booking – a dirty studmark in an otherwise surprisingly clean game. Rush loses it. He's screaming at the referee, still shouting as Molby waddles up and floats in free kick short of pace but long on guile that brushes just wide, with Lukic rooted bamboozled to the spot. And Rush is still shouting at the ref.

While Liverpool are showing early signs of break-up, Arsenal are beginning to discover a sense of shape. Hayes and especially Davis are beginning to assume some sort of command of midfield. Anderson is beginning to adventure forward a lot more out on the right, wing-back style as space begins to open up all over the field. He gets behind Whelan, picks up the ball, gets into the box – but a second or so after being dispossessed innocuously, dives spectacularly to universal merriment. The ref tries to keep a straight face as he has a word in Anderson's shell-like.

The play's beginning to spread from end to end. Suddenly, Hayes finds the Liverpool defence breaking before him like clouds and a shaft of sunlight showing him the direct path to goal – but a wave of self-disbelief seems to overcome him and he fumbles the chance as Liverpool regather. McMahon shows him how it should be done, striding straight back with a direct run through midfield culminating in a low, grasscutter that slithers just wide.

Charlie's almost alone upfront as Liverpool begin to gather a head of steam – but it's John Lukic, sometimes iffy on crosses, who gathers the ball assuredly off the head of Spackman as he tries to get on the end of a Craig Johnson cross.

Now it's Arsenal's turn as Davis begins to direct matters from midfield. Davis to Rocky, who tries a one-two with Nicholas that doesn't quite come off. Then the ball breaks back to Nicholas who advances, crablike across the Liverpool penalty box in search of an opening. He unleashes one, it bounces off Hansen's chest. Nicholas picks it up again out on the left and manages to wriggle through a tight guard of Liverpool's defenders like a cheeky punter oiling his way past two burly bouncers on a night-club door. He's in the box – but then he trips, apparently over his own bootlaces. No penalty. None asked.

It's untidy stuff but disconcerting to Liverpool. Anderson again has a country squire's luxury of depopulated acreage to himself out on the right. He pulls it back to Nicholas who skews badly, his worst shot of the day, a diabolical sitter. But Liverpool aren't out of the woods yet. Arsenal are still peppering. A game but routine cross lands with a plonk in the Liverpool six-yard box and Whelan and Grobbelaar make a slapstick music hall turn of picking it up ('After you, me ol' China!' 'No! After you, gov'nor!') before Niall Quinn slides in and almost manages to connect with the stray ball with his long legs.

Nicholas is still in there. Once again, he seems to worm his way through what can't be more than an inch of space between Venison and Johnson out on the left and this time wins a corner. In it comes – and he blazes over the bar, almost bringing down the overhead TV Zeppelin. But he's not discouraged. And Liverpool aren't coping.

Twenty minutes to go and two tactical changes. Kenny Dalglish brings himself on in place of Paul Walsh, to martial his troops. Respectful applause and much remarking in the commentary box about why he doesn't pick himself more often. Dalglish, legend of the modern game, who like Nicholas made the trek down south from Celtic although, most observers would agree, did so with rather more success. He's now player/manager, in his mid thirties but his wise head and incisive cool in front of goal could be just what turns this game. The General is in the field. Now the Arsenal dervishes mush be quaking. Charlie was certainly in awe of Dalglish – his boyhood idol, his tongue practically tied itself in a knot the first time he tried to speak to him man-to-man in the Scotland dressing-room.

Dalglish canters on to a hero's welcome, takes up a commanding position upfront, glides infield as a chance develops – and, for no apparent reason, falls flat on his back. He gets up, laughs ruefully and issues a general apology to fellow players, fans, even viewers watching at home. It's the only contribution he will make that afternoon.

George Graham makes his move around the same time. He pulls off Quinn and sends on young Perry Groves, a funny-looking little fellow with Tin-Tin ginger hair, a ruddy face and the general air of an agitated hamster. He was George Graham's first signing for the club, picked up at a snip from Colchester. The sort of player that managers like, who scurries about a lot. No one seems unduly disquieted by his introduction. Big mistake. This has been George's masterstroke. At once, Groves introduces a bustling flash of energy for which Liverpool seem to have no answer.

He's barely been on a couple of minutes before he's glanced a header half a yard over the bar. A game that was showing signs of petering out into an understanding between the teams that they carry on the fight in extra time has now come to life again. The Arsenal end prick up. Seconds later, Groves is clean through but hauled back, marginally offside.

Eight minutes to go. A throw-out from Lukic to Samson, who, in the inventive spirit of all England international full-backs, pumps the ball hopefully up the left channel. Only this ball's going somewhere. Groves, legs still fresh, scuttles the extra yard to claim it. He's away, up the wing – he skips over and past Gillespie, leaving the Liverpool defender in a pile on the touch-line. With three of Liverpool's back four advancing menacingly on him, as he cuts into the box he spots Charlie loitering persistently on the edge of the box, neglected in the panic over the little hamster-man. Groves cuts it back to Charlie but Charlie seems to have made just the wrong shape to receive it. He's off balance. No he isn't. He catches it on the outside of his right foot. Now everyone else is off balance, including Whelan who tries to intercept but ends up deflecting the ball just enough to look back in despair as it trickles past Grobbelaar sailing in utterly the wrong direction on an acrobatic but futile dive. One-nil down, 2-1 up!

Just five minutes to hold on – but already it's all-singing, all-flag waving pandemonium at the Arsenal end, a writhing, cockney cakewalk. The diffident-looking Martin Hayes is pulled off, replaced by the young Michael Thomas, whose day of destiny would yet come, to shore up in midfield. Last throws of the dice for Liverpool. John Wark, who once appeared alongside Pele and Sylvester Stallone in *Escape To Victory*, the hilariously appalling football movie, is frozen on the touchline, waiting for the call of 'action!' to sprint on for the last three minutes for Liverpool, and, who knows, a last-gasp Hollywood ending.

You'd expect out-and-out nuclear assault in these last few minutes but Liverpool seem to sense the game is up. The third-formers exhibit amazing brashness in the face of the defeated prefects. David Rocastle and Paul Davis do a little encore of snazzy triangular passing movements in the middle of the field, culminating in an almost insolent Charlie Nicholas backhell that very nearly puts Perry Groves through. It's encore stuff, cheekily reminiscent of Leeds Utd years earlier when they beat Southampton 7-0. But Liverpool aren't quite finished. They're lofting balls in, Arsenal are heading them, punting them back. Alan Hansen drifts forward and launches one. Dalglish passes –

but Ian Rush fails to connect and, with no one within five yards of him, dives into the penalty box. Even the Arsenal defenders look embarrassed for him. Everyone does the decent thing and pretends this risible incident never happened. This was to be his triumphant last hurrah before flying out to join Juventus. But instead the spell of the talisman has been broken. A week later he would score against Norwich. Liverpool lost there too.

Into stoppage time . . . but there haven't hardly been any stoppages. The final whistle blows and, as Liverpool players freeze where they stand, stunned and crestfallen, the Arse go ape.

Bob Paisley, Liverpool manager and good old Corinthian, bounds out and congratulates the Arsenal team members individually. This game has been contested in a remarkably good spirit, just the sort of advert the game needs. Amid the usual delirium of players wrestling each other to the ground, George Graham strides out on to the pitch among his charges, like an indulgent headmaster on playground patrol turning a blind eye to high jinks on the last day of term. Though headline writers will dub this the 'Nicholas final', he can smile quietly to himself in the satisfying certainty that it was Perry Groves, his first signing, and his decision to throw him into the ring late on, that turned the game.

As for Charlie, it's cha-cha time. 'It would be fantastic to score a couple of goals at Wembley . . .' Well, he has. Ironically perhaps the two worst goals he ever scored, but so what? Just and tardy compensation for all those spectaculars that hit the woodwork during the frequent goal droughts in his Arsenal career. The day it counted, he rose to the occasion, as fervently hoped. Throughout the 90 minutes he had been, by turns, typically infuriating, inspiring, ineffectual, incisive. But he had won. When it mattered, when it came down to it, Charlie was a winner, even if all he'd won thus far was the hearts of the Highbury faithful. And now Arsenal had their first trophy in eight frustrating years. In the continuing wrangles with George Graham that would determine whether or not he would remain basking in the glare of those oft-mentioned bright lights of London, he had won himself crucial bargaining kudos.

The message in the tabloids the next day, with Charlie holding the Littlewoods trophy defiantly aloft, put it bluntly, 'Sell Me If You Dare!'

But had he done enough?

Chapter Two

Charlie Nicholas was born in Scotland on December 30 1961, just 24 hours before Hogmanay – Charlie was never one to miss the party, unwarrantably cynical wags would later quip. The middle one of three children – older sister Janice, who would later come down to London and flatshare with him when he became homesick, and younger brother Stephen, who would attempt to follow in Charlie's footsteps, his parents were mum Rena and dad Chic, a former PT instructor who later joined the *Glasgow Herald* as a print union official. Charlie was brought up in Maryhill in Glasgow on a modest council estate. Thumbnail sketchers would later go into wistful, Hugh McIlveney mode when discussing Charlie's upbringing, reaching into the cliché box to describe a bleak but romantic world of gritty tenements, cobbled backstreets and gritty, hard-bitten experiences down the mines, etc.

None of this was really true of Maryhill. Although it was a working-class area it was certainly not deprived or rundown. The state Charlie was brought up on was known as the Barracks as it had been built inside the boundary wall of the old Army depot where unstable renegade Nazi Rudolf Hess had been interned having parachuted into Scotland with a view to negotiating a peace with Winston Churchill. Otherwise, nothing out of the ordinary.

Charlie's upbringing was a solid, warm, loving and unpretentious one – he would always set a high premium on his family background, even in the daft, heady days of the mid eighties.

Moreover, coming from a mixed, Catholic-Protestant background, Charlie would never have had any truck with the sectarian nonsense for which football in Glasgow had become a catalyst in the small minds of some people. An early questionnaire in the *Celtic View* when he had just broken into the first team put it rather nicely. 'LIKES: Baked beans on toast. DISLIKES: Bigotry in all its forms.' There you had the lad.

He was typically football obsessed – green and white to his marrowbone. It was ingrained. In an area where hoofing around a football was for many kids the dominant form of social intercourse, he not only loved the game but loved Celtic with an abiding passion. And there was a lot of love. In 1967, when Charlie was just six, Scottish football had hit a zenith of pride. It wasn't just that the national team had beaten England, the World Cup holders, putting the Sassenachs to flight with a performance that was almost mockingly overwhelming. At club level, Celtic had won every trophy they competed for, including the European Cup where, after dominating the second half, they had run riot over a churlishly defensive Inter Milan side with a bedazzling, revolutionary eight-man attack formation, including the likes of Bertie Auld, Bobby Murdoch, Jimmy Johnstone, Bobby Lennox and the indefatigably Tommy Gemmell, securing a 2-1 victory which would make them the first British victors in tournament.

To Celts, this victory would be the stuff of Homeric legend, with the 'Lisbon Lions' commemorated in boozy reminiscences for years to come, of Gemmell's rubber-legged, mazy excursions down the left flank, of Steve Chalmer's deflection for the winning goal, of that bloke in the grey socks and kilt who stood on a wall and led the Celtic chant throughout the game. They almost – indeed, ought to have – done it again in 1970, when, after overcoming Leeds in an enthralling, two-legged semi-final (thereby answering a lot of questions about the alleged superiority of football south of the border), they were caught napping by Feyenoord in the final.

Nonetheless, under the aegis of the late Jock Stein, Celtic were absolutely dominant during that period, continuing so into the early seventies, with the arrival of a free-scoring young talent named Kenny Dalglish. The legacy of those years to modern-day Celts is at once a source of immense pride, and on the other hand a burden, building up high expectations which subsequent Celtic set-ups have all but torn themselves apart trying to live up to.

None of this would yet be a worry for Charlie. He, like most youngsters, idolized Kenny Dalglish, whom his father would take him to see every week down at Parkhead, a long-established appointment in the Nicholas family. 'My father used to take me to what we call the Celtic End and sit me on the barrier as early as six or seven. I was fortunate because I watched the Lisbon Lions here. I saw greatness and success and entertainment. That's what I've had with the supporters. I think I look for the same things they look for.'

He'd spend hours kicking a ball against a wall in emulation of his hero. 'When I was young, all anybody talked about was Kenny,' said Charlie. 'I was fanatical about him. I was never the type to model myself on anyone but I always watched everything he did very closely. How do you describe what your boyhood idol means to you?

'Every time Kenny didn't have the ball I felt this urgency . . . just give Kenny the ball, I'd be screaming.'

Years later, many Celtic fans would feel the same towards Charlie.

At school, Charlie was remembered by some as a 'quiet, reserved' boy. However, when a football was dangled in front of him he came scampering out of his shell and developed a fizz and precocity that would spill over into all aspects of his character. He made his mark as a wee prodigy in the local Maryhill leagues. So good was he indeed that he was often picked for teams of older kids, playing well above his age group.

There may be things that the average male adolescent dislikes more than being humiliated by a younger, smaller boy, but offhand it is hard to think of any. And young Charlie was tactless enough to leave boys older than him dumped on their backsides in the mud as he twinkle-toed past them. Very often his victims would retort in the blunter footballing language of the two-footed, studs-first tackle from behind – which is why it was as well that Charlie had himself a 'minder' in the burly shape of long-standing friend and neighbour Jim Duffy, today manager at Hibernian. Whereas to this day, Charlie is known to the world as Charlie and Jim as Jim, to each other they are 'Charles' and 'James'. Charles and James had an understanding. If anyone of the pitch came after Charles and clobbered him, then James would go after the clobberer and clobber him. It was a simple arrangement and word soon got round that anyone who was of a mind to leave their boot imprints on the boy Nicholas would shortly have the boy Duffy to answer to. Pat Crerand, apparently, played a similar 'minding' role for George Best – perhaps there were times later on in his career when Charlie could have done with that sort of looking after.

By the age of just 11, Charlie had joined up at Celtic Boys' Club. Strangely, however, it was to be some time before he made a real impact. Too diffident, perhaps, to argue for a place he felt really comfortable in, he struggled for some time in the unlikely role of sweeper, where it had been somebody's bright idea to try him out. This would later give him sound grounding in the development of his all-round abilities, but the idea of Charlie Nicholas doing a sort of responsible, policing job behind the back four seems about as appropriate as putting Gary Lineker in goal.

Eventually, the penny dropped and Charlie got his chance; and by the age of 15 he was lavishing goals with all the spring-time abandon of the Easter Bunny dispensing eggs. Scottish sports writer Jackie McClean later recalled, albeit with 20/20 hindsight, the first time he saw Charlie. 'It was during an Eastercraigs tournament (an annual event which shows off the best schoolboy players). There was a Paul McStay there, also one Paul Nicholas. Then there was Charlie. His first touch was when he trapped the ball. This is one of the most basic moves in football. Don't ask me how but I knew I was looking at the sort of talent we hadn't seen in years.'

Charlie signed an agreement whereby he would train every week at Celtic Park, with the club officials keeping an eye on him, monitoring his progress. However, on leaving school at 16, he briefly took up a trade as an apprentice motor mechanic. After just a few months, however, Celtic persuaded him to sign up for the club proper and ditch the exciting world of dirty valves and replacement exhaust pipes for the more mundane prospect of becoming a flamboyant Celtic legend in waiting. It was a wrench, naturally, but after about 15 seconds of careful consideration, Charlie signed up.

His mother Rena, initially, was against it. She was aware that for every ten or so young lads signed up by these big clubs, only about one was likely to make it, with the rest thrown out the back door with little regard for the fact that they would have to go back, cap in hand and face the man they'd six months earlier told where he could shove his apprenticeship and say, er, is that job I left still going?

It wasn't just that Charlie was losing the chance to develop an unexciting but nonetheless steady trade. She sensed that young Charlie was about to fly the next into a giddy world of temptation and pratfall. It would be a while, quite a while, before she felt entirely certain that Charlie had done the right thing.

Charlie's was a typical footballer's apprenticeship – much scrubbing of boots and laundering of shirts. There were, however, occasional junkets such as a Boys' Club trip to America where he met the godlike Pele, by then in his late thirties and playing for fun for the New York Cosmos during a brief vogue for soccer in the US which evaporated as quickly as it erupted. A photo of Charlie then, looking rather chubby around the chops and stricken with boyish adulation, still survives. One of the Celtic staff then remembers Charlie back then as a bubbly bundle of fun, 'always chatting, always singing'. He also recalls that during their sojourn, Charlie befriended a young spastic boy: 'Charlie would spend hours with the lad, rolling around with him on the floor, taking him for walks.' Then, as now, doing charity work was a staple part of club PR with players volunteered, reluctantly or otherwise, for hospital visits and the like. Charlie always threw himself into such work with great enthusiasm and frequency, as those who know him attest time and again.

Charlie also experienced two brief spells in England – years before the bright lights of London beckoned, he would venture down for footballing spells on secondment in the rather dimmer lights of Ipswich and Wolves. The reception he got, especially in the latter town, might easily have put him off anywhere south of the border for good.

He and another lad who had accompanied him down for the duration decided, on their first night in the West Midlands, to stroll out and take in the sights of Wolverhampton. Having fairly quickly surmised that Wolverhampton consists basically of a sequence of roundabouts and not much else, they were about to head back when they were accosted by a bunch of local lads. Whether these lads took offence to the Kevin Keegan perm Charlie was in the process of growing out, whether there was something about his cocky, happy-go-lucky demeanour, or whether they were just bored with counting roundabouts and fancied a bout of recreational, mindless violence against some lads smaller and less numerous than themselves, it's impossible to say. The upshot was, however, that they each produced flick-knives and gave chase to Charlie and his pal through the dismal, dark, rain-sodden town precincts.

Later in his career Charlie was often criticized for lacking an extra half yard or so of pace but not that night. He ran for dear life, as did his mate, eventually taking breathless sanctuary in a shop, from where they managed to put a call into the police and get an escort back to their digs. It's unlikely that Charlie would have been eyeing Steve Bull's number 9 shirt longingly in any event, but after encountering that particular welcoming committee it was still less likely. He got back up to Scotland the moment he could.

Charlie, had he but known it, was only months away from breaking into the first team – but he still regarded himself as an ardent fan rather than a player in waiting. Every week was the same – meet up with the chaps, and then down to the Jungle, the large hangar-cum-barn that had been hastily erected on the site of the original wooden stand that had been burned down, probably deliberately, in 1904. With its low roof and concrete floor it might have seemed to the neutral observer, when empty at any rate, to have all the congeniality about it of the sort of quarters reserved for cattle shortly before dispatch to the abattoir. But to Charlie and thousands like him, the Jungle, 'warm, noisy and green', was in every sense his own section of Paradise. Each week he would willingly share in the communal surges of rapt anticipation, the deflated groans, the tides of noise rising to explosions of euphoria. So brief was the transition between Charlie the fan and Charlie the player that when he started scoring regularly for Celtic he would still keenly feel the symbiotic link between himself and the terrace.

'It's not just arriving at the stadium. It's when you leave the house. Meet up with your mates, travelling down on the bus together, knowing your father was going down with his mates, there's a constant sense of atmosphere . . . you've really got something to look forward to in life. And it was Celtic. And that was the same for thousands of people. I was in the Jungle for every game. And when I scored I could easily imagine how fans would be celebrating that goal,' said Charlie.

Like the great Dixie Deans before him, he understood, and continued to understand, what it was to be a fan.

However, he hadn't quite made the transition yet. There were still boots to be blackened, shirts to be folded. His last game as an out-and-out fan was on May 21 1979. The season had been extended somewhat due to an arctic winter which wiped out Scottish fixtures during January and February. Celtic had looked unlikely to overcome their Old Firm rivals Rangers in the

Scottish Premiership, especially having lost to them 0-1 away just 16 days earlier. But the unseasonable extension of the Premiership schedule seemed to be a filip for Celtic and they had won three out of their remaining four rescheduled matches. Their last fixture was against Rangers at Parkhead and the title, in Brian Moore's immortal phrase, was up for grabs now.

Charlie's last job during the day was to prepare the kit for the team. That done, he was away – but not before he failed to resist the temptation to nick a few official first-team jerseys to wear to the match that evening, one for him and some for his mates, including Willie McStay. Buried deep in the throng of 52,000 that balmy, barmy evening, they wore their ill-gotten acquisitions with pride during the game, a classic for those of a hooped-green persuasion with Celtic, reduced to ten men, running away 4-2 victors thanks to goals from Aitken, McCluskey and a last-minute 20-yard cannonball strike from MacLeod. It was the perfect evening, described by the Celtic chairman as the club's finest night since 1967 in Lisbon. Charlie and pal stood proud in the Jungle, as close to the front as they could get. Unfortunately, Celtic decided to reciprocate the salute. They did a lap of honour culminating in a lengthy bow in front of the Jungle – with Charlie terrified. Why? Because there he was, Charlie the ground-staff boy, on open display in his purloined first-team jersey. This, remember, in the days when most supporters wore sensible clothes and confined their adoption of team colours to their scarves. In actual Celtic shirts, Charlie and his pal would have stood out like a prize pair. In what should have been the crowning, euphoric of his days as a supporter, with Celtic having snatched the title from their rivals at the death, Charlie was wishing he could be invisible. If any of the players spotted him, he would be in it up to his neck. And sure enough, Tommy Burns of all people espied poor Charlie and grassed him up.

Charlie had to take a carpeting – but it wouldn't be long before he was wearing the shirt for real. Things were moving quickly. In the 1979-1980 season he would gravitate to the reserves and notch up a very handy 25 goals for the second team, catching the eye not just of those within the club but also the keen-eyed monitors of the *Celtic View*, the weekly magazine dedicated to the club and its affairs. All of those on the inside track enthused about the new wunderkind in their midst, 'quick and elusive on the ground with a keen sense of the oppositional goal'.

It was more than mere cultish enthusiasm that prompted Celts to advance the cause of Charlie, however – there were those who felt that it wouldn't be a bad idea for the prolific young striker to be given his chance in the first team, because Lord knows, they needed somebody upfront. Celtic had led the Premiership for most of the 1979-80 season but they'd always had Aberdeen snapping at their heels. After years of making do with whatever bronze was going while the Old Firm routinely squabbled over the gold and silver, the Dons, under the steward-ship of Alex breaking up the traditional Glasgow monopoly. This was the first of Fergie's red reigns and would eventually culminate in Aberdeen's winning the European Cup Winners' Cup but for now they were sniffing after their first League title in living memory.

Come the end of March and the wheels were still attached to Celtic's challenge. During the month of April they would fall off, one by one, in four calamitous defeats, including a 5-1 home defeat at the hands of Dundee (Dundee!) which reduced players and manager Billy McNeill alike to psychological bathchair cases. Quite what had gone wrong most people were too shell-shocked to surmise but it was clear that something, anything, needed to be done.

McNeill, however, resisted frequent and voluble calls to put Charlie in the first team. Though Charlie had by now turned 18, McNeill judged that it might be detrimental to his nurturing and development to plunge him into the frenzied last furlongs of a title race. 'I fought against myself not to put him in the first team,' McNeill would say later. Maybe he should have let himself win. He paid the price for caution – Celtic missed out on the Premiership by a point. League championships, however, weren't exactly a once-in-a-generation occurrence for the Bhoys. There was always next year and the year after that. The summer break would enable young Charlie to come on still further and then, perhaps, they could think about elevation to the first-team squad, who knows, perhaps even a place on the bench.

By the end of the season, Charlie was clearly outgrowing the reserves, scoring with such ease that it was becoming embarrassing. He eventually had his first run out for the first 11 in a 1980-81 pre-season friendly against a less than crack team of German amateurs dredged up from some tributary of the Rhone as cannon fodder – 10-0. Curiously, Charlie failed to get among the goals.

No matter. McNeill had decided to bring the boy on, and

Danny McGrain was nominated as his off-field 'minder'. McGrain, a veteran hero at both club and national level, a gruff, solid defender who had earned universal admiration for coming back from injury – a skull fracture – and, though a protestant like Jock Stein, would remain a loyal servant to Celtic until 1987 when he left the club, unforgivably unheralded, on a free transfer. A proud, determinedly bearded and orthodox Scot, it fell to him to pick up young Charlie from his parents' home in Maryhill every Saturday, with his father having cooked him the three hot dogs he always prepared him, superstitiously if not entirely nutritiously, before matches. It fell also to Danny to deliver him to training sessions and generally take him under his wing, encourage him in the various do's and don'ts of professional football.

Temperamentally and in any other respect you might care to imagine, Charlie and Danny were poles apart – but they seemed to get along all right, with Danny shaking his head in uncomprehending despair at Charlie's latest stylistic excess of ludicrous trinket (Charlie had long since abandoned the folly of his Keegan perm and had adopted a New Wave wedge cut), while Charlie would chide Danny for still knocking about in his demob gear. It was impossible not to like cheeky, puckish, pisstaking Charlie, once you got to know him.

Manager Billy McNeill shared Danny McGrain's sense of exasperation. 'I look at some of the things that Charlie wears at times and I just shut my eyes and wonder,' he said. 'But I couldn't take grievance with him; he's cocky and arrogant and he has an infectious sense of humour.' His effervescence was all the frothier now that his dreams were on the point of blooming into bright green reality.

On September 9, 1980, Billy McNeill finally relented to the almost anguished cries to give Charlie his chance. The competition was the Scottish League Cup. The opposition would be modest – Stirling Albion – but still more modest had been Celtic's performance against these supposed minnows in the first, away leg where they'd managed to lose 1-0, their self-belief evidently about as low as where they'd left it at the tail end of the previous season. Charlie would be on the substitute's bench, champing at the bit, dying to uncork his best.

Celtic embarrassed themselves still further at Parkhead, conceding yet another home goal. But they managed to reinvoke some semblance of their proud tradition and, with a late goal, saved their blushes and doubtless a barracking, forcing the issue to extra time – and thank God the away goals rule didn't apply. Having at last relaxed a little, they finally remembered that they were Celtic F.C. and not a bunch of inept clodhoppers who happened by coincidence to play in hooped green jerseys and surfed home on a wave of relief with four goals in the remaining half hour.

And here it was that Charlie got to give an exhibition. On this, his début, he joined in the romp with two great goals, one of which, a curling, 20-yard shot from outside the box would provide a taster of the panache he was about to bring to Parkhead.

The fans went ape. A legend had been born. Bonnie Prince Charlie, St Nicholas, Cheeky Charlie, had arrived.

Chapter Three

Those goals against Stirling Albion weren't a one-off. Or even a two-off. Five days later, Charlie made his Premiership appearance. This time, the opponents were Partick Thistle. It was like watching a promising young boxer being gradually brought on against increasingly less mediocre opposition. He scored another pair, one of which was typical of the breathtaking cheek that would be his stock in trade. On the edge of the box, surrounded by a menacing thicket of Partick defenders with a 'none shall pass' air about them, he simply lobbed the ball over the top of them into the net, the keeper evidently taking a fag break assuming his services wouldn't be required at that particular juncture. The crowd, especially the younger element, loved it. It was as if he was taking the mickey.

Further appearances and more goals followed against Herts (2-0) and Airdrie, where Charlie demonstrated a cool and poise beyond his years by volunteering and successfully executing penalty duties. Rave reviews compared him to a continental player, the continent still being a distant place where tanned limbed maestros performed magic arts with the ball, usually at Celtic's expense as they crashed out in the early rounds of European competition. As Hearts stalwart and (briefly) Celt himself John Colquhoun remembers, 'There was always such excitement, such freshness about Charlie whenever he played – it was the kind of thing that we look for these days when we import foreign players. But Charlie brought it in from Scotland – he was one of the boys as far as fans were concerned.'

Charlie knew all about the continent as he'd been to Benidorm. But the quick-thinking, quicksilver style he brought to the game, the sense of fun and cheek and unpredictability and bunking past defenders had a swaggering, buccaneer, dare one say it, post-punk feel about it. But a little more of that later.

As magazines began to profile Charlie, they discovered that there was an extra string to his bow of newsworthiness – he was a bit of a dandy. Glasgow, like a lot of unlikely northern cities, was basking in the neon glow of the New Romantic era. There was a vogue among the young, in places most laid waste by the brutal cutbacks of the early Thatcher years to respond, not with a reassertion of cloth-capped working-class pride but with an implicitly sarcastic determination to dress UP! The worse the recession hit towns like Leeds, Sheffield and Glasgow, the more their young came out clubbing in toppers, tuxedos and baggy pantaloons, an ironic response to the tide of rising unemployment and post-industrialism. Charlie's sister Janice was one of many 'trendies' who got about in that era – it's to her that some of the credit goes for awakening in Charlie his fashion-consciousness.

Scottish football had never had a dandy as such. Kenny Dalglish had been somewhat of a hero, to say the least, but his dress sense more or less amounted, insofar as anyone bothered to enquire, to standard-issue flares. Jinkin' Jimmy Johnstone was revered as a God in elfin shape by Celtic lovers but the way he wore the token amount of hair fate had granted him generated few, if any, column inches. Okay, there'd been Peter Marinello, Scotland's own Charlie George, but he had been so fleeting and ephemeral a footballing presence he was all but forgotten.

Here was Charlie, by contrast, posing for Scottish newspapers in the sharpest, bang-up-to-the-minute outfits a man of still relatively modest means such as himself could afford. 'Here's Charlie the dapper Etonian in Bidermann grey flannels and double breasted Paul Boye blazer at £59.95' gushed a typical blurb. And these, let us remind ourselves, were the days when £59.95 meant £59.95.

What seemed most to disconcert the authorities was Charlie's flagrant disregard for sockwear, the wearing of. One might have thought that with all the myriad problems besetting Scottish football at the beginning of the eighties that sock inspections would have been pretty low on most managers' list of priorities. But no. Charlie himself preferred to wear no socks – by necessity, he claimed, rather than affectation. 'I spend most of my money on clothes,' he explained. 'And that means going without socks in some casual outfits.'

Socklessness being considered a breach of some arcane details of professional footballing etiquette, however, Charlie complained that he was forced to walk around with a spare pair of socks in case his assistant manager caught him at the club baring his ankles for shame – whereupon, if reprimanded, he would have to nip into the gents for a quick socks change.

What's more, Charlie had been spotted frequenting Glasgow's burgeoning nightclub scene. Nightclubs! Nightclubs with disco-dancing floors in them! With people disco dancing! With Charlie disco dancing! He was Glasgow's top disco dancer, twinkle toes Charlie! Well, perhaps he didn't actually dance but he'd certainly been spotted standing at the edge of dancefloors. Drinking. Drinking himself senseless! Had to be carried out of the place. Well, maybe not, but he certainly had a drink in his hand.

Such was the hype and rumour that Charlie's attendance of after-hours nighteries triggered off. Whereas these days agents piratically take registers to ensure their young charges attend the requisite after-hours venues, in the early eighties it was considered pretty exotic for footballers to be caught in hot nitespots. In the sixties, there'd been vague attempts to marry Peter Osgood and his Chelsea cronies down the King's Road with the whole mood of Swinging London but time and perspective would soon reveal that he and his fellow professionals were merely blokes who liked a drink. George Best certainly set the tone for the footballer as playboy and there were obviously attempts to present him as a leading edge figure in the pop zeitgeist but again, once the smoke had cleared, it was pretty plain that he was part footballing genius, part sorry, philandering alcoholic and victim of dodgy marketing schemes.

Whether it was truth or fiction, however, the fact was that

there had never been anyone quite like Charlie north of the border. Somehow the idea of a Scottish footballer going to a sawdust and dominoes pub and drinking themselves into a quiet stupor was considered well and good, rugged and orthodox – but poncing about in nightclubs!

Later, the curiosity regarding Charlie's off-the-field lifestyle would come to pester him but for now, it was all innocent, colourful fun and good copy. Young women, who were yet to take a significant demographic interest in football, began writing in to Scottish papers celebrating Charlie's technical assets. A sense was growing that here was emerging the makings of a pop footballer.

On the field, meanwhile, Charlie was continuing to dance through defences. At the beginning of October 1980 he came up against Aberdeen, nemesis of the previous season. The result was a 2-2 draw, and Nicholas scored again. He'd yet to fail to score in a first-team shirt this season. The next week against Dundee he found the net once more. Scottish journalist Kevin McCarra would later reminisce with great relish about the young Charlie during this period, who 'treated the game as one long invitation to take the ball and torment another player'.

Poor little Morton were wheeled on, the next set of stooges – followed by Kilmarnock, thrashed 4-1, with two Charlie Nick penalties converted with customary swagger and aplomb.

Then came Rangers, Charlie's first Old Firm clash. In the context of those few, heady weeks it must have seemed like the final examination.

Chapter Three

Meetings between the two teams weren't exactly rare now that the new Premiership meant that clubs met each other four times a season. On top of that, they'd inevitably bump into each other at least once more, usually in the latter stages of the League or Scottish Cup. No one on either side, however, was ever blasé about these occasions, which seethed with an atmosphere all their own.

Pete Davies, interviewing Terry Butcher in his brilliant *All Played Out*, his study of the 1990 World Cup, conveys as well as anybody the cauldron of fervent partisanship that makes for a Celtic-Rangers clash. Davies recalled a visit to Ibrox, the venue where Nicholas would make his début, 'There were 42,000, three stands of blue against one of green – and the outpost of green was awash with Irish tricolour. An awesome noise of defiance rose up from among them – and when the players came out the sound in the whole place was volcanic, totally deafening . . . you felt the glory and the animal both stirring in your gut. The noise never seemed to stop; and the game started off at 200 miles an hour.'

Hatred spilt over. Local celebrities, such as ex-Skid Richard Jobson, an avowed Celtic fan, found himself gobbed at in the face when he set foot in the stadium by Rangers fans. Terry Butcher told how he had willingly gone native when he signed for Rangers, so seduced by the bitter euphoria that he chucked out all his U2 and Simple Minds albums. The 'Gers were the more rigidly Sectarian of the two teams – the 4 Be 2's indie rock anthem 'Why Don't Rangers Sign A Catholic?' posed the pertinent question with lyrical unsubtlety but admirable directness.

Celtic could be just as bad, however, with their tricolours, rebel songs and 'evil chants' of a pro-IRA nature which, while only the preserve of a tiny minority as a rule, swelled to more like a majority for old firm clashes. In the early eighties, in the wake of Bobby Sands and the H-Block protests, sectarian emotions ran higher than ever. After the Falklands War, it was even the habit of some fans to chant pro Malvinas songs (the Argentinian moniker for the islands) as proof of their anti-Unionist, anti-establishment stance.

No one was chanting about the Falklands in 1980 but the level of enmity between the rival teams was still feverish. Back in the previous May, after the Celtic-Rangers Scottish Cup Final, which Celtic won 1-0, there had been riots at Hampden Park when Celtic fans spilled over the fences to greet their team at the King's Park End, after the team had, unwisely in the view of the authorities, gone over to give a victory salute. Rangers fans duly burst the cordon and swarmed on to the pitch at the other end and, as ever when the kids are united, the upshot was inevitable – they beat the tar out of one another, until baton-wielding police intervened.

Wounds of resentment were still fresh as Charlie and co took the pitch that November afternoon. Charlie himself had no sectarian impulses. How would he cope with the atmosphere?

He didn't. He froze. He had a nightmare. Although in retrospect it probably had less to do with the atmosphere and more to do with the attentions of one Derek Johnstone, a former striker himself, now winding up his career as a centre back. He marked Charlie out of the game – and marked him, too, with a couple of, so to speak, vigorous challenges. After that, Charlie took fright and didn't care to know too much more. When asked in an interview shortly before this game what his impressions had been of Premiership football, Charlie Nicholas had replied, with an ill-advised hint of cockiness, 'It hasn't been as physical as I imagined it'd be.' To one or two defenders, that remark might well have been taken as an invitation to come and have a go if they thought they were hard enough. It was certainly physical enough now, and then some. Billy McNeill was forced to pull him off.

Celtic were scattered to the four winds that day and ran off 3-0 losers. Said Charlie later, 'I had no experience of anything like that atmosphere so the game just ran by me.'

In fairness to him, the whole team played with all the firmness and personal conviction of green jellies in a high wind – they were characterised as 'timid and uncoordinated' by one observer. But for a while at any rate, a question mark would now hang over the Bonny Prince. Had he lost his bottle? Was he just a delicate fancy Dan who didn't fancy the job once the crunching tackles came in? Or was it just one to chalk up to experience?

A 0-2 drubbing at the hands of Aberdeen the following week didn't help either – so thank goodness the obliging Airdrieonians were up the week after, light duties, giving Celtic the chance to regather themselves, bolster their nerves and engage in some target practice. Charlie registered with a penalty in a 4-1 victory but in the sterner challenge of the two-legged Scottish League Cup semi-final, Celtic crashed out 4-1, a Nicholas goal insufficient to save their hides.

Ever since he'd made his début it had been more or less of a conga upfront for Charlie but now he was being administered one or two small doses of adversity. One of the little knocks that would hamper his playing career put him out of action for a month and he disappeared from public view for a few weeks, but at least the heat was off. He reappeared in late December to slam in a consolation goal in a 4-1 drubbing at the hands of Aberdeen. Come Christmas, Celtic were in need of all the wishbones and lucky sixpences they could lay their hands on.

Billy McNeill had his work cut out galvanising his psychologically befuddled men and over the Yuletide interval he got down to it. Players were called in for a series of barrackings, geeings-up and cajolings. Celtic, they were told, could not be content with second best. He adjusted training so that greater emphasis was put on sharpness and speed. Celtic had been overrun too many times. No one would catch them napping now. All of this played perfectly to Charlie's strengths, freeing him up to develop an upfront relationship with Frank McGarvey, his striking partner, formerly of St Mirren, who had gone down South and had a fruitless spell in the Liverpool reserves before returning to Scotland for a then not insubstantial £250,000 transfer fee. McGarvey was the perfect foil to Nicholas, a busy, workmanlike striker, though in his own way just as puzzling to opponents as Charlie – McGarvey could control the ball like it was tied to his bootlaces.

After Christmas, the transformation was as miraculous as a New Year's resolution actually upheld. Nicholas and McGarvey were now engaged in a private, friendly battle to see who could hack it most effectively upfront. McGarvey was certainly doing the business in terms of quantity – he put four past Kilmarnock and Morton as Celtic quickly gathered momentum. But Charlie, whether as goalscorer or goalmaker, was always a jewel to behold, a player for whom the challenge of beating defenders seemed as much a relish as actually scoring – there were times when, having passed them, he seemed in two minds as to whether or not to go back and have another go at them as opposed to go for goal.

Celtic picked up maximum points in January but then the inevitable big freeze put them on ice for a few weeks. Cometh the thaw in late February, however, cometh the Rangers. This time at Parkhead. This time, Charlie was ready.

There is no greater joy, no more dramatic a delight in sport than the comeback challenge, the reversal of fortune. In athletics, one thinks of Sebastian Coe coming back to beat Steve Ovett to gold in the Moscow Olympics of 1980 in the 1500 metres, having been left scrambling for silver days earlier in the 800 metres. In boxing, of Sugar Ray Leonard, who'd suffered a humiliating bruising against Roberto 'Hands of Stone' Duran, coming back only months later and jabbing, poking and Ali-shuffling his old nemesis into an extraordinary eighth-round defeat, when Duran simply turned away and conceded the fight. Or Joe Louis, badly beaten by wily heavyweight Max Schmeling a few years earlier, pulverising the German in one round in 1938 in what many saw hopefully as a metaphor for the coming war. Or in football, England, beaten on penalties by Germany in 1990, coming back in 1996 in front of their own crowd and turning the tables as

Southgate blasted it into the top corner . . . well, this is sport and such morality play happy endings are never guaranteed.

Nothing was guaranteed for Charlie as he stepped out that day – if he froze again against the 'Gers, a hoodoo would descend on him, the sort of mental block that footballers notoriously superstitious, find hard to shrug off. But he was feeling sharper, quicker, looser limbed, the end spark of a livewire spirit that was running through the whole team.

'The dressing room was full of characters at that time,' recalls Danny Crainie. 'Davie Provan, Tommy Burns – and especially Charlie. He was always singing, jabbering, winding players up, making calls from outside, pretending to be another manager, that sort of thing.'

Celtic were on song while rivals such as Rangers and Aberdeen seemed temporarily to have lost the hymn sheet. It was looking good. Surely.

Not in the opening stages though. Doubt descended like a clamp on Charlie – he didn't look good. He hadn't shaken the curse. He wasn't getting the run of the ball. Then, it broke in the box. Charlie was there, or thereabouts. Instinct took over from inhibition and he lunged forward with a toepoke. Goal!

It was ugly but it was beautiful. The second was more elaborate, more worked, as he took it inside the penalty area, seemed to run it too far – then in one impossible swivel snatched a goal from the maw of hopelessness. Celtic eventually ran out winners, 3-1 . . . This one wasn't for himself but for the fans, the giddy, glad, mad band of hope in the Jungle – it was as if Charlie could still feel himself in there among them, baying and cheering, as he scored the winning goal, looking out at himself.

After that, the rest of the Premiership season was a cakewalk. Celtic was in the driving seat and so was Charlie, who, having just passed his test, was presented with a Vauxhall Chevette, no doubt a prestige vehicle in that long ago era, by grateful sponsors who were just now getting an inkling of this boy's potential marketability.

By April, the title was practically in the bag – so long as they took care of the small matter of beating Rangers away. For Charlie, pause for thought. Sure, he'd managed to get on the winning side of an Old Firm clash, but that was at home, among friends, in the green warmth of Paradise. Now he was back to Ibrox away – and Charlie, sensitive to places, didn't need reminding that this had been the site of the worst game, the worst moment in his brief career. What was more, the Scottish press had warned that any player who scored had best not gloat and leap about too much as they might bring the current Old Firm tension to flashpoint.

Celtic could take nothing for granted. They'd hiccupped in the Scottish Cup, losing to Dundee in a semi-final replay in spite of two Charlie Nick goals. Aberdeen who, under Alex Ferguson were growing in strength by the year, hadn't give up the fight – they were still in with a shout, although a surfeit of draws was hampering their progress. The game was not a classic, agreed neutral observers (if there ever were such a thing in Glasgow), a hard-fought, scrappy, niggly affair, as 'untidy as an upturned ashtray' in the words of one reporter. Though by this time Rangers were effectively out of the running it went without saying that nothing would have given them greater pleasure than to urinate on the bonfire of the Bhoys, Celtic, too, were naturally tense and come half time the scores remained level in an atmosphere simmering with anxiety and expectation.

Ten minutes into the second half, things hadn't opened up much. Then Pat Bonner, long-serving Celtic and soon Republic of Ireland goalkeeper, Jock Stein's last signing before he departed, gathered up a dud shot and threw the ball out to Davie Provan, much loved servant to the club whose career would eventually be cut short by illness. Provan negotiated his way up the wing, taking on and leaving Dawson in his wake before setting up an elaborate one-two with Frank McGarvey, who dummied the Rangers defence before returning the ball to Provan, now on the edge of the penalty area. The Rangers' defence were wrong-footed for once, leaving a hole for Provan to advance into, before slipping it to Charlie Nicholas, on the balls of his feet, biding his time as ever, waiting for that split-second that sometimes only occurs once in 90 minutes to seize on his opportunity. This was it. Surrounded by blue-shirted foes he managed to find the leverage and angle he needed and blasted the ball past Stewart into the back of the net. Indescribable, head-to-toe rush of blood, adrenalin, endorphins and joy. But no excessive celebrations. 1-0! Danny McGrain made a bee-line for Charlie, smothered him with a bear-hug and hauled him away from the glaring daggers of the Rangers end.

After that, Rangers came after them with shotguns, like hillybilly fathers whose daughters had been abducted by out of town folk. They had been stung – and pride and honour were at stake.

The next 40 minutes were not comfy for Celtic and they were forced to pull their wagons into a circle in their own penalty box as Rangers surged forward. Right at the death, Rangers looked from all sides to have struck home with the equaliser – but Roy Aitken cleared off the line, guaranteeing he wouldn't have to buy any of his own drinks that evening. Finally, three sharp blasts from the referee's whistle – music of the spheres. Celtic were all but assured of the championship, Charlie had wiped away all doubts about his ability to handle the big occasion and the banners said it all – 'CHARLIE IS OUR DARLING!'

The championship was finally secured for certain at Tannadice Park, a goal from Tommy Burns providing the clincher, and Celtic could afford to take their foot off the pedal as they eased home, championship winners by a full seven points over Aberdeen – they'd registered a record 26 victories and 56 points, testimony to a positive, goal-hungry approach personified by Charlie, who, though he ended the season with 28 goals – one fewer than partner McGarvey – was voted Player of the Year by fans.

Danny Crainie has glowing memories of Charlie in that heyday, 'He was one of the most skilful players I have ever seen. It wasn't that he was quick – he just threw the defenders with movements of his body. And his touch and control of the ball were unbelievable.'

Charlie started the next season in typically rampant form – two goals in a 4-1 defeat of Hibernian, including one spectacular volley, and an overall study in panache around the penalty box. He greeted fans with his now-customary Native American war dance, a typically engaging characteristic which prefigured the obligatory routines that greet every Tom, Dick and tap-in these days. The terrace salute – a lowing 'Char-LEE! Char-LEE!', sung to the tune of Big Ben's chimes, provided a further sign that interest in Charlie was beginning to develop into rather more than conventional warm affection for a 20-plus goals per season striker. The sound of the distant flapping of cheque books south of Hadrian's wall was beginning to register in the rumour mills of Glasgow's pub scene. Arsenal, it was said, were having Charlie watched – their scouts had been on hand to see him drive home the winner against St Mirren in October. Liverpool were interested too. They might even be prepared to splash out to the tune of seven figures. All of this was a source of pride rather than disconsternation. The Sassenachs could gaze longingly but it couldnae touch. After all, no way would Charlie move away from Celtic, from home and hearth and Paradise, not for all the gold in the Bank of England.

The cult of Charlie was gathering pace. As he notched up his 50th appearance, a newspaper article pointed out gleefully that at the same age as Charlie, previous Celtic legends such as Kenny Dalglish, Lou Macari, Davie Hay and John Connelly had only managed a few games between them, let alone made any impact on the scoresheet. If 30 goals this season, the implication was, then why not, say, 50 next season? The Charlie phenomenon seemed destined to grow and grow unchecked.

Also growing and growing unchecked was Charlie's hair, now in its third stage of evolution – from Keegan perm, to smart wedge to flourishing Bonoesque mane. The Irish group U2 were just beginning to make their first impact around this time with hits such as 'I Will Follow' combining a rising sense of passion, ringing guitars flowing freely like adrenalin and a post-punk smartness – the musical equivalent, you could argue, of Charlie's football. Indeed 'I Will Follow' was the track Charlie would play on match days to galvanise himself, get his blood up. Never had a Scottish footballer, or Scottish football, chimed in so conspicuously with the goings on in the music world. Great as the Lisbon Lions of 1967 had been, no one had ever even thought of suggesting that theirs was psychedelic football.

In November 1981, London got their first glimpse of Charlie Nicholas as he came down south to participate in, of all things, the *Daily Express* five-a-side tournament. An annual event, this always threw up eccentric results and giant-killings with big teams affecting, at any rate, not to take the whole affair entirely seriously. Charlie, though, was up for it. In spite of the continuing bouquets flung his way, he'd been having a slightly lean time of it in the opening months of the Premiership. McCluskey and McGarvey had been forming a prodigious scoring partnership upfront and Charlie, now sporting a number 7 shirt, had only racked up a couple of goals and was reduced to the substitute's bench. He was hankering for a bit of netbusting.

Had five-a-side ever attained serious sporting status, like, say, table tennis, it may have been Charlie's true forte. No having to bust your lungs covering every inch of the turf, exhausting yourself pointlessly. Here, it was a simple matter of taking on your man at close quarters, swerving and jinking through the most improbable of gaps. Mind you, Charlie would have missed the terraces.

Whatever, Charlie and co wiped the wooden floor with the opposition, slaughtering a Man Utd team that included Bryan Robson, Ray (still then 'Butch') Wilkins and Frank Stapleton 5-1, before meeting Southampton in the final and seeing off a team that included Alan Ball and Kevin Keegan 1-0. *Sportsnight* viewers in England would have had agreed with a knackered Keegan's judgement that Charlie ran them ragged.

Up north, however, things had tapered off. Lacking match sharpness through over-attachment of backside to substitute's bench, he hit a brief, fallow period and as the season turned the Christmas corner, he was back down in the reserves, where Billy McNeill hoped he might recharge his batteries. And so it was that, one freezing, January afternoon Charlie found himself as far away from the mass gaze of adoration as you can get – hacking about on the bone-hard pitch of Morton's Cappielow stadium. Dallying on the ball deep in Morton's half, he was playing one of his teasing games with opposition defenders, slipping the ball through to colleague Jim Dobson. But he couldn't skip over burly Jim McLoughlin's incoming tackle – and, as a spasm of pain shot through him like none he'd ever known, he keeled and splatted on to the hard ground.

Charlie had broken his leg.

Chapter Four

The Morton injury could easily have finished off Charlie. Or certainly shaken him so badly he would never be the same player again. No longer would he feel that he led a charmed life on the pitch, his quickness of thought, cunning, cheek and guile leaving him immune to the studded boots of opposing defenders. It was commonly suspected that rival Premiership managers had already wised up enough to Charlie to send out defenders charged with the task of 'doing' him at the first available opportunity – and while no one was suggesting that there was any malicious intent in the Morton incident, now he knew he could be 'done' and, worse, what it felt like to be done.

The trauma of the break stayed with him for years. In the nineties, when back at Parkhead, he had a wretchedly quiet game at Morton. He later explained that he'd been fazed by the fact that this was his first visit back to the ground ever since that hideous day in January 1982 – the injury had long healed but traces of the mental scare still niggled.

Anyone who imagined, however, that the young Charlie could be crushed like a butterfly with a boot was soon to be disabused. His irrepressible character, his itchy feet, above his will to play football, combined in him to set him on a course of recovery that amazed onlookers with its speed and determination.

The break had been a clean one and it was hoped that Charlie wouldn't be out of action for too many months. The Celtic physio immediately put Charlie to work on a programme of exercises designed to keep him physically active, building up his shoulder and stomach muscles. Moreover, Charlie of his volition spent hours hobbling up and down the terraces of Parkhead in plaster to stave off the rust. Through those cold, early months he made excellent progress. By the end of March his plaster had been removed and by April he was said to be two to three weeks ahead of schedule in his recovery programme. The moment the Doctor gave him the nod he was back in training and in his first match after injury, a reserve game, he came on as substitute and scored a ludicrously incontinent seven goals.

In some respects, the broken leg had been a blessing in disguise. Scottish elders in the football world certainly approved of the fact that Charlie, through blessed adversity, had learned that life can be stern and earnest and that we are not put in this vale of tears for mere gallivanting and gadding about alone. More importantly, through his new programme of upper body exercises, Charlie had built up sufficient strength to ensure that, while he'd be no barrel-chested charger scattering defenders in his wake, that at 5'9", he had sufficient poundage about him to hold his own a tad more sturdily.

All of this would stand him in good stead as he prepared to embark on the 1982/83 season which most would rank as his finest ever, in the finest Celtic team in years, the season in which, as Celtic's official history would have it, Charlie Nicholas 'seemed to be waging a one-man campaign against Scottish goal-keepers'.

His first game of the new season was against lowly Arbroath in the Scottish League Cup final and Charlie was soon bulging the net when a Roy Aitken run and assist set him up for a left-foot drive. What's more, his overall performance was an indication that, in spite of his bitter experience, his footballing feet were still dancing to songs of sprightly innocence, 'Charlie's broken leg has not sabotaged the mischievous character, the skilful improvisation or the thrilling improvisation around goal – he still has about him his impish personality, his cockiness and cheek' reported the *Celtic View*, the official Celtic magazine.

Fair enough, it was only Arbroath but Celtic set a green blaze in those early rounds of the League Cup that were scorching by any standards. Nicholas, who would go on to score in every remaining match of the competition, put four past Dunfermline as Celtic racked up a total of 23 goals in six preliminary round games.

They swept past Partick Thistle 7-0 on aggregate, the latter finding that trying to stop Celtic when they were on this sort of charge was like trying to flag down *The Flying Scotsman*. In the semi-final, however, they came up against Dundee United. They dispatched them tidily enough at home but at Tannadice took their eye off the ball and found themselves 2-0 down with two minutes to go. Whereupon Tommy, sensing Charlie on the prowl upfield, delivered the perfect pass, leaving Charlie heading north just as the Dundee United defence were heading south. McAlpine between the sticks had been caught too far forward and Nicholas duly chipped the stranded keeper with studied impudence, to make the aggregate score 3-2 and book Celtic a place against, of all clubs, Rangers in the Scottish Cup Final.

By now, Charlie had come to relish these cosy little clashes. His attitude to Ibrox defenders was becoming akin to that of Bugs Bunny towards Yosemite Sam. He loved nothing more than to turn them inside out until the steam came blasting out of their ears with frustration. But Celtic had had a relatively barren run in the Scottish League Cup, not having won the competition since 1974.

December 4 was a day of driving wind and rain – relatively pleasant by Scottish standards, leading to some early worried talk of climatic shifts and global warming. Celtic were certainly quick to raise the temperature, taking the game to Rangers from the start, a fluent, green wave of assertive, attacking football, culminating in a forward move in the 22nd minute. McStay managed to extract the ball from a committee of Rangers defenders, linked up nicely with Provan, who cut into the box and then back to Nicholas, rapidly approaching down the middle. Nicholas collected the ball without breaking stride and, judging his moment perfectly, paused to wait for a gap roughly the width of a football to open between a cluster of defenders, the goalkeeper's outstretched hand and the far post before firing. 1-0!

Celtic added a second after Rangers failed to clear their lines and Murdo MacLeod pounced – but the 'Gers replied short after the second from a freekick and from thereon in to the final whistle it was muddy trench warfare. But Celtic held out, sodden to the skin but happy, happy.

Highlight as this was, a still higher light had illuminated Celtic's season a few weeks earlier, at the end of September. Celtic's fans had become wearily accustomed to their team's revolving door fortunes in European competitions – they'd been dismissed by Juventus last season in the first round and the season before had suffered the indignity of being bested by Poli. Timosoara, East Europeans ordinaire, in the Cup Winners' Cup. So when Ajax of Amsterdam came to Parkhead and forced a 2-2 draw, no one troubled to entertain any illusions about what was in store for Celtic when they travelled to Amsterdam. Billy McNeill had criticised some of his players for showing Ajax too much respect, containing as they did such stars of the past as Johann Cruyff and stars of the future as Marco Van Basten, to say nothing of such cultured Danes as Olsen, Lerby and Molby.

Celtic maintained level terms thanks in part to a Charlie Nicholas penalty but when running after the Ajax stars it was a moot point as to whether the Celtic players intended to tackle them or ask for their autographs.

The return leg was to be the stuff of misty-eyed legend. all that remains on celluloid of that night in Amsterdam is black and white video footage culled from Dutch TV with accompanying Dutch commentary. Yet somehow it's almost better than the images of what took place that night are so grainy, sepia'tinted and indistinct, much as they live on in the memory of those who still celebrate them.

Haring forward in numbers as if chivvied by McNeill's exhortations, Celtic had Ajax rattled like so many thoroughbreds startled by a rampaging pack of hounds. But the supreme moment of style, grace and audacity belonged to Celtic Nicholas. With 34 minutes gone, Graeme Sinclair surged forward down the left channel and passed to Charlie, who took the ball on the edge of the penalty area, skipped blithely across one tackle, leaving the Ajax defender flat on his face chewing turf, before laying the ball off to McGarvey. With him he worked the deftest of one-twos, then, just as it looked like he'd twisted himself into a knot, the Ajax defenders closing in and seemingly having got him bang to rights, Charlie delivered a left-footed chip shot that almost raised a divot, sending the ball sailing past the flabbergasted Schrivjers, into the net, as the Ajax defenders tumbled on to their backsides and hammered the turf with frustration. Two twists, a flick on, a lob and there it was, a goal true Green-blooded Glaswegians still raise a glass to even now.

Pat Bonner insists that he had hinted to Charlie that he'd noticed in training at the ground the previous day that there was a weird slopy bit in the Ajax box which Charlie, should he have gotten the chance, might care to use as a tee-up against the keeper should he find him stranded. Still, a little of the credit for the goal should go to Charlie.

Ajax equalised in the second half but Celtic stuck at it, tails up. McGarvey hit the bar – then up popped Charlie Nicholas again, setting up the chance for substitute McCluskey to score from 20 yards out. 2-1 on the night, 4-3 on aggregate and a European performance that replenished Celtic's self-esteem on the international circuit. Ajax were the *pièce de résistance* of haute cuisine – yet, remembers fan James Payne, 'Charlie made Jan Molby look like a big pudding that night.'

Meanwhile, in the Premiership, Celtic were flying, with Charlie Nicholas once again leading the charge. 2-1 against Kilmarnock didn't quite rank with the laying low of Ajax but one of Charlie's two goals was a solid gold deposit in the memory bank – with his back to goal, he turned, shot and scored in one intuitive, instant swivel.

Of course it wasn't just Charlie Nicholas – Celtic had an embarrassment of options. There was young Paul McStay, Davie Provan, McGarvey and McCluskey, Roy Aitken and Murdo MacLeod, all of whom were capable of the sort of teasing, exciting, confrontational football which recalled the spirit of the Lisbon Lions. And Tommy Burns who would pop up with the occasional offering such as a Brazilian-like effort against Dundee.

But Charlie it was who was best loved of all, and Charlie who, in spite of the competition, was finding the back of the net with almost frightening frequency. The *Scottish Daily Record* annually awarded a crate of champagne to the player who was first to reach 30 goals in a season. With plenty of shopping days left until Christmas, Charlie could already lay claim to the bubbly. Herein lay the origin of the 'Champagne Charlie' tag, one he was to have subsequently difficulty living down, or a lot of fun living up to, depending on whose opinion you canvassed.

Charlie was becoming increasingly difficult to ignore. He appeared on *A Question of Sport*, a chirpy presence amid the pullovers and laboured middle-England humour – he lost, to Willie Carson's team. He continued to add to his goal tally though. Celtic heads were beginning to chatter excitedly of his eventually breaking Bobby Lennox's career total of 168 goals or even, holy of holies, the legendary pre-war maestro Jimmy McGrory's 397 goals, hitherto considered a spire of unassailability. On reaching 37 goals, with the season far from over, a *Celtic View* statistician felt that there was sufficient range and quantity to make a proper analytical breakdown of the total. This revealed the extraordinary fact that although Charlie was a natural right-footer, his preferred choice on the nine out of ten penalties he had successfully converted, of the goals in open play, he had scored 15 with his left foot as opposed to nine with his right.

His natural facility with either foot was never better illustrated than against Rangers in January of 1983 when, in the words of Scottish journalist Kevin McKenna, Charlie took the 'Gers defence on 'an alternative tour of Ibrox' dragging the ball speedily from one foot to the other, bewildering the opposition like a street hustler urging the punters to guess which cup the dice is under, before zipping off at a tangent, and hooking in a disingenuous, floated left-footer over the Rangers keeper whose attention was still on where Charlie had been at yards ago. The delirium that this goal, perhaps his finest Old Firm effort, induced in the crowd behind the goal was comparable with the sort of crowd scenes that met the Ayatollah when he returned to revolutionary Iran from exile.

Charlie had the freedom of Parkhead – but troubling signals had reached the rumour mills. English clubs were making eyes at Charlie. And word was, Charlie was making eyes back.

Chapter Five

On the field, Charlie was a Godsend to Billy McNeill. Off the field, he was becoming a bit of a headache. Over the past few months, Charlie's media profile had slowly begun to heighten. To begin with, it had been photos of Charlie next to lucky lads from the Celtic fan club meeting their idol, Charlie meeting the sisters of St Joseph's hospital in Edinburgh to present him with a £1000 cheque. Nice.

Then one or two odd ones started to creep in. Charlie advertising, of all things, fitted kitchens. Then it was Charlie looking fetching in a sleeveless tank-top. All the time he was wearing the same, well-meaning, irresistible, anything-to-oblige smile as he had worn for the nuns. In a funny kind of way, the affable, anything-to-oblige spirit that prompted his numerous charity appearances also prompted some of the naffer, more tabloideazy photo-ops that would come his way over the next few months.

With the first stirrings of a feeding frenzy in the offing for Charlie's transfer signature, the media began to put a magnifying glass to the newly-christened Champagne Charlie. Champagne Charlie who spent his spare hours coiffuring his barnet. Champagne Charlie who hung out at clubs, a pirate of the small hours in his cutaway t-shirt and sporting an earring, eyeing up the girls and basking, according to one writer, in the 'ear-splitting din of Kajagoogoo and The Thompson Twins', two spiky, funky synthesizer bands of the early eighties, now both long forgotten. Such antics make for quaint reading but at the time, this sort of thing seemed like the sleazier goings on in the Cities of the Plain.

It was the earring, as much as the socklessness which seemed to agitate Billy McNeill. He cracked down, imposing £10 fines every time he caught Charlie out of standard-issue blazer and slacks. Charlie knuckled down like a good lad – but in the meantime, his frequenting of Glasgow's club scene, his penchant for a drink, a laugh and a bit of the other, were being monitored from a distance by jealous fellow Glaswegians, a mixture of Rangers fans eager to land Charlie in it, aghast Celtic fans who wondered what effect all this high living might be having on his training programme and jealous geezers, maybe lads who'd been on the brink of trials themselves but never made it 'cos their faces didn't fit, y'know, who felt that the least Charlie Nicholas could have done, having made it as a footballing superstar, was to observe a strict regimen of parsnip juice and celibacy. One such character, so a story goes, once came tottering bolshily up to Charlie in a club and started giving him verbal – 'You bloody so-called stars, you're not so big. I can do anything you can do, pal, anything!'

To which Charlie replied, 'Oh, yeah? Can you do this, then?' Whereupon he took out a £20 note and tore it up in front of the guy's face. The punter stumbled off, speechless – and Charlie picked up the bits of the £20 note and Sellotaped them together later at home.

Glasgow has always been a goldfish bowl – back then, as now, if you wanted to go out for a bit of a night on the tiles, you only had a handful of places to go. Ultra Tech, maybe, or Henry Afrika – although recent changes in the licencing laws had made Glasgow a relatively hip and happening place compared to a few years previously. For anyone who fancied a night of Charlie-spotting, anyone who wanted to grass him up to the big man, it was a piece of piss. There were always stories about Charlie getting drunk here, picking up a woman there. He used to run around with a 'rat pack' that included Danny Crainie, Mick Conroy and Willie McStay. Like the time when Danny McGrain had given the lot of them a lift to some club after an evening's drinking to return home to the relatively sensible and mature company of his own children. Back home he got out the car, opened the boot to fetch his kit – and out rolled Charlie.

'We lived life to the full,' remembers Danny Crainie with a chuckle, 'but we trained hard as well.'

All the same, Billy McNeill would arrive in his office every morning and find a pile of letters and phone messages offering details of how Charlie had been living it large, oot on the tap, disco-dancing drunkenly from one hot spot to another.

Suspicions were further inflamed when Charlie was dropped from the Celtic line-up that faced Aberdeen in the semi-finals of the Scottish Cup in 1982, a match they were to lose 1-0, due to what even the soberest of Celtic history books drily refers to as a 'mysterious injury'. That Charlie played – and scored in – matches days before and days after this fixture settled the matter in the minds of freelance speculators in the Glasgow pubs that there was some other explanation for his absence than Charlie's own,, loudly protested explanation that he had suffered an injury. He'd been suspended, reckoned some. Too hungover to train, sneered another.

It certainly hadn't helped matters that Charlie had picked up a drink-driving conviction recently – damn that Vauxhall Chevette! Yet he protested, not unconvincingly, that he was just like any normal young man of his age. He drank, he clubbed, he shagged, but all in moderation – well, perhaps not the latter. Asked point-blank by one early tabloid interviewer exactly how many young women he had, so to speak, stepped out with, Charlie erupted with giggles, then, on calming down and giving the question serious consideration, realised, that at the age of 21, he had quite lost count.

Whatever the explanation for the Aberdeen incident, the final proof of Charlie's constitutional adequacy was out on the pitch and there, if it was champagne that was flowing through his veins then to hell with the medical experts, it was doing him the power of good. Four goals in three games against Dundee United (twice) and Hibernian kept Celtic in the running for the title. As speculation began to mount about his future, however, as the spotlight of the media trained longer and more frequently on him, Charlie became the victim of the surly resentment of oppositional defences, the niggles getting sharper, the crunching tackles still crunchier. Having limped off midway through a 4-1 drubbing of Kilmarnock back in March, Billy McNeill felt duty bound to make a futile appeal to the latent pukka spirit in Scottish defenders to go easy on the lad, lay off with the rough stuff. He might as well have appealed to the men of Glasgow to lay off the hard stuff. The tackle from behind was still legal in Scotland and this became one more reason on Charlie's 'for' list to leave Scotland, with the number of 'againsts' dwindling. He was getting kicked to pieces on the pitch, torn off a shred off it and running the gauntlet of Glasgow's bitter-drinking, bitter-minded element.

The strongest inklings that Charlie might be heading down south began to emerge at the beginnings of 1983. By this time, Charlie had acquired himself – or been acquired by – an agent. A former bankrupt, Bev Walker had gone on to try his luck as a would-be boxing promoter, with a stable of several likely prospects – until he shied away from the sport, disabused by what he euphemistically described as the 'politics' of the boxing game. A chance meeting with Brian Jacks, the judo star who'd managed to broaden his media appeal through appearances on BBC's *Superstars*, led to his setting up a sports agency, that would soon go on to handle the affairs of former gymnast Suzanne Dando, cancer victim turned Grand National-winning jockey Bob Champion and swimmer Sharron Davies.

Walker was becoming wise to the possibilities of diversification he and his stable of photogenic sporting types might be able to enjoy. Charlie first met Bev Walker through Brian Jacks in a meeting at the Glasgow Holiday Inn and they had soon agreed terms.

In Charlie Nicholas, Bev had found a commodity who, like Jimmy White in snooker, had a haircut to match a mannishly brash, go-ahead attitude, who cut a romantic dash and had a little of the rogue about him – yet also possessed a winning smile, an engaging charm, and, most importantly of all, was young, ambitious and would do anything to oblige. Billy McNeill was to find himself in an increasingly impossible position. Like many a manager to come, he was forced to deal with, even share interviews with Bev Walker, an agent, with interviewers forced to deduce from McNeill's granite-faced, stoic reserve, just what he thought of Mr Walker, who, leaning back in his chair and adopting an expression of bland serenity, quietly realised that the more goals Charlie scored, the more interest grew in him, the hotter a property he became. He was a rapidly appreciating asset.

'I have a working relationship with Billy McNeill,' said Walker. 'Certainly, our business has started to infringe on football matters but he is a realist about it all.'

In the press, Charlie wasn't talking any more about how he wanted to be the new Kenny Dalglish – now, he was set to be the new Kevin Keegan, the new George Best. The playboy image he'd inadvertently triggered off, a myth, a construction which Bev Walker had gently egged along with photo opportunities of Charlie adopted all manner of rakish, stylish postures, was beginning to appeal. And on the field he could continue to do no wrong.

The sea of rumour was filling with sharks, quiet predators, and red herrings. Tottenham were supposedly interested. Or maybe not. There'd been enquiries from European clubs. Supposedly. Billy McNeill, increasingly quizzed by the media about Charlie, found himself on the horns of a contradiction. On the one hand he explained how dearly he wanted to keep Charlie, even build a team around him. Yet on the other hand, his every comment about his young protégé was the sort of glowing blurb in which estate agents specialise. He was doing an unfortunately good job of selling Charlie to the world.

'How good is Charlie? He's the best. Possibly the most exciting young striker Scotland's produced in ten years. People talk about Dalglish but Charlie has a greater media rapport with the public than Dalglish. He's the most exciting young player I've ever seen and, if he left, no amount of money would compensate Celtic,' said McNeill.

The more he talked up Charlie, the more likely it became that he would move away from the club. Of course, by now, he was probably already resigned to the fact that Charlie would be on his way and was simply pitching to get the highest price. But the truth was that Billy McNeill would dearly love to have held on to Charlie. When he said that no amount of money would compensate for losing Charlie, he sincerely meant it. He fought a rearguard action to the last, insisting that he was in negotiations with Charlie, that he would offer him the most attractive terms possible to stay – but from early on, the writing was on the wall.

In the midst of all this transfer speculation, Charlie was on the point of making his big breakthrough in the Scottish national team. He'd already picked up Under 21 caps and naturally, with his personal ratings high among supporters and his phenomenal scoring rate, there was a countrywide clamour for him to be included in the Scottish squad alongside his boyhood idol, Kenny Dalglish. Jock Stein had been strangely reluctant to pick members of the Celtic team these past few months, in spite of their riotously successful league campaign. Could that have had anything to do with the bad blood he still harboured towards Celtic, after the shabby way in which his departure from the club had been handled?

Whatever, Stein now found himself faced with an injury crisis, with his preferred strike force Robertson, Steve Archibald and Alan Brazil all out. There was a friendly coming up against Switzerland – Charlie's name was in the frame. Stein, grinding his teeth, reluctantly admitted the possibility that yes, yes, maybe the boy Nicholas had a shout.

One thing would always be for certain, however – Jock Stein didn't much care for the likes of Charlie. Since he suffered that tragic, fatal heart attack moments after seeing his Scotland side overcome Wales to qualify for the 1986 World Cup, stressed out by a badgering barrage of press photographers, Stein's legacy and reputation have been practically carved in stone. Twelve years on, venerated Scottish journalist Hugh McIlveney would profile him on a TV documentary as a man whose colossal, monolithic qualities of character had been forged by his experiences down the mines, where he had remained a worker almost into his mid-twenties. There he had had instilled in him hard and enduring lessons about the virtues of team-work, solidarity and man-

management that would stand him in terrific stead during his playing and subsequent managerial career. He had not shot to immediate stardom like young Charlie Nicholas but had grafted arduously to earn his spurs, first as a part-timer at Dunfermline before eventually working his way, slowly, steadily and solemnly up the sheer rock-face to the pinnacle of his success. Jock Stein was a sober, steadfast, Protestant, autocrat with short shrift for frippery and flibbertigibbets.

In other words, what he made of a young, green, long-haired little rascal like Charlie Nicholas who reportedly had interests in a hairdresser's, swigged cocktails in poncy nightclubs, posed for photos for London newspapers, nipples shamelessly bared, and pranced about in Italian slip-on shoes to the likes of A Flock of Seagulls was probably unprintable. And what he thought of agents you could probably glean from one glance at the back of his head. But, though it must have galled Jock Stein to the core of his being to admit it, Charlie did seem to have a knack for hitting the back of the net.

So it was that at the end of March, Charlie Nicholas found himself lining up in the tunnel to take the pitch for Scotland against Switzerland. Kenny Dalglish would line up alongside him, leaving poor Charlie in a state of awestruck palpitations. But Dalglish, always a player's player rather than a charismatic public figure leaned over and whispered, 'We're all equal now.'

Those little words of encouragement did the trick. A largely uneventful game was brought crackling to life by a memorable moment of vintage Charlie Nick in the 75th minute. Managing to get on the end of a cross-field ball, he brought the ball down with one foot and scored with the other, without the ball even hitting the ground, while defence and keeper were caught waiting for him to go through the motions of trap, steady, take aim and fire. The match was of little consequence but his market value shot still further through the roof. John Wark, looking on, described Charlie's performance as 'frightening'. Charlie, meanwhile, flushed with national pride, refused to swap his shirt at the end of the match.

Meanwhile, the transfer latest continued to bubble over. Manchester United joined Liverpool and Spurs in the cauldron of speculation. Don Howe at Arsenal was watching too. Liverpool angered Billy McNeill as word reached him that they were planning a £1m double coup, scooping up both Charlie and Paul McStay. 'No one will make a deal with Nicholas ahead of me. I am appalled at the ethics of Liverpool,' he shouted, but the more he protested, the greater the sense grew that events were overtaking him.

The Italians joined the fray in earnest, their attention grabbed by that volley against Italy. Inter Milan, Juventus, Roma and Napoli were all reputed to be interested. The *Daily Mirror* speculated that Charlie might become a 'lire millionaire' at the rates they would be offering. Poor financial advice, as a million lire back then would have amount to about £800.

Hard as it was for Charlie to keep his concentration, there was still to settle the matter of winning the Premiership title. Celtic had let themselves go slightly and Aberdeen were once again breathing down their neck. Alex Ferguson had done a good job of motivating his players, firing them up by developing a siege mentality in them, always telling them how the Glasgow media had a bias against them. Perhaps they were over-inflamed – there was one dressing-room clash after an Aberdeen player had jeered 'Fenian bastard!' at a Celtic opponent.

With only a few games left, Celtic had thrown away two games, one in which they snatched a 3-2 defeat from the jaws of victory against Dundee United, a second when they lost 1-0 to Aberdeen. They fought back with victories against Kilmarnock and Morton but with one game to go, Celtic found themselves equal with Aberdeen – but a point behind Dundee United, who had managed to sneak through the leading pair unsuspected and now led the table.

The final game of the season was against Rangers. Dundee United were up against Dundee the same day while Aberdeen would face Hibs. It would go right down to the wire.

Celtic made a bad start, trailing by two goals away at Ibrox and all seemed lost, as fans, transistors pressed against ears, learned that both Aberdeen and Dundee United were up winning at half time. Somehow they mustered the energy for one, final, death or glory, roar-and-be-damned charge, the Celtic fans raising the decibels behind them, and came back with a mighty swag of four goals, including two clinical Charlie Nicholas penalties. And yet, they needed yet one more, one more and the hope that Dundee might equalise against United. Go! Go! Final whistle . . . doh!

Unbelievably, after putting together some of their most exciting, most fruitful football in living memory, having notched up 90 goals in the Premiership alone, with Charlie Nicholas alone having scored over 50 goals in all competitions, after that legendary night in Amsterdam, after all that flair and passion and cheering until their lungs were fit to explode, all they'd walked away with was the League Cup.

The growing realisation that Charlie Nicholas was on his way merely compounded Celtic misery. There was resentment in some quarters – all he'd given the club, moaned some, was a single season, a solid apprenticeship and now he was bogging off down to some fashionable English club to reap the benefits. These feelings journalist Phil Gordon describes as those of a 'jilted lover' – for a youthful love affair is what the Jungle had had with Charlie Nicholas, an infatuation – but when the time came to consider marriage, long-term commitment, he was away. Bastard!

But Celtic's nagging sense of dissatisfaction ran deeper than that. Sure, in the last five seasons alone they'd won the Premiership three times, they'd won the Scottish Cup and League Cup – but somehow it didn't seem enough. Maybe it was that the legacy of Jock Stein loomed too large, like the massive portrait of him that hung over the manager's chair, or maybe it was a rarely articulated but deep-down felt realisation that this was only Scotland, after all. An average of a mere trophy a year practically constituted failure. What about Europe? Sure, they'd beaten Ajax but only to be knocked straight out in the next round by Real Sociedad. And that had been a relatively good showing. Generally, Celtic found themselves dumped on their behinds by some tinpot team from a tinpot nation with an unpronounceable name. Celtic hadn't even reached the semi-final of any European competition since 1974. Where was there to go? Where was the ambition?

Charlie too, sensed this lack of ambition. It was of some consolation that if Celtic were bad, Rangers at that point were even worse – since that calamitous first appearance at Ibrox in 1980, Charlie had never been on the losing side in any Old Firm clash. But again, so what? Attendances told their own story. October 30 1982, 60,408 watched Celtic beat Rangers 3-2. A fortnight later, 15,044 watched Celtic beat St Mirren 5-0.

As Charlie was voted Scottish Player of the Year, Manchester United barged into first place as favourites to sign up Charlie, with manager Ron Atkinson, all champers and cigars and front, making sanguine noises. It was official now – Charlie would be leaving Celtic on the expiry of his contract. Charlie, who was now writing a ghosted column for the *Sun* as Bev Walker carefully guided his commercial interests, openly admitted that Manchester United were his own team of preference. Man U were a big club with a grand tradition, especially of signing Scottish footballers. At Liverpool, however, he felt he would be 'chasing shadows', specifically those of Messrs Keegan and Dalglish. Even after the latter's avuncular reassurances in the dressing room before that Scotland international, Charlie still felt paralysed with awe in Kenny's presence. A heavy-hearted Billy McNeill commented, 'The fact that the speculation is over is no relief to me at all. There isn't another Charlie Nicholas in the country.'

But the speculation had only just begun. Newcastle now joined the runners and riders, along with Arsenal. A further complication arose as the Scottish football authorities announced that they would expect any differences over the matter of Charlie's transfer fee to be settled by the Scottish tribunal system, which involved negotiations between an English, Scottish and 'neutral' representative. Liverpool's Bob Paisley began to cool on the whole deal. He'd throw in his offer and that was that. 'We don't like being kept waiting by tribunals,' he growled, truculently. Ron Atkinson seemed a little cooler all of a sudden, too. 'It's difficult to see where I could play him,' he remarked, as if this difficulty had only just occurred to him. More to the point, it was difficult to see what he could pay him with – Man U, yet to strike upon the idea of own-brand lager and changing their kit every fortnight, were reportedly in debt to the tune of £2.6 million. Charlie was at this point temporarily unavailable for comment – he'd been booked in to judge a Miss *Evening Mail* contest and then he was due to co-commentate for Radio Two on the English FA Cup Final. And appear on a chat show to discuss men's fashions. Bev Walker was keeping him busy. Weeks later, however, Charlie would write that, on meeting Ron Atkinson he had been unimpressed by his flash, brash demeanour: 'He came on far too strong. He talked more about himself than Manchester United or me.'

Days later, with still nothing firmly decided, British tabloid reporters clocked rather an alarming sixpenn'orth of Charlie when he flew into London a couple of days later for talks with a top London club, reputedly Terry Neill's Arsenal. But what did he look like?

Charlie's dress sense had long been a lively addition to the gaiety of nations. His penchant for earrings, signet rings and jackets worn with the sleeves rolled up in accordance with early eighties fashion mores, all of this the sartorially conservative sportswriting establishment had taken on the chin. And certainly, while his dress sense would have struck anyone in 1983 under the age of 23 as especially avant-garde, though admittedly quite good for a footballer, photos of Charlie from the era don't stand up too well today.

Once, it was seventies fashions we laughed at – billowing flares, hot pants, stacked shoes, tight tank-tops. In the nineties, however, a 'so-naff-it's-good', affectionate, tongue-in-cheek attitude towards these aberrations crept so far into the fashion mainstream that nowadays, seventies revivalism is now integral to any hip nineties ensemble. These days, early eighties gear – shiny strides, rolled up sleeves, hair longer at the back than on top, white shoes – all looks unforgivably naff. In other words, the eighties are the seventies of the nineties. Follow?

Back in 1983, of course, the seventies were still considered a recent embarrassment, the decade that style forgot and the sort of natty, Italian-inspired, modish togs Charlie sported would have been mostly regarded by clothes commentators of the day as fashion getting back on track and then some, over-compensating for the sins of ten years ago. Chic, yes; daring, yes. Laughable? Certainly not.

The leather outfit in which Charlie arrived at Heathrow airport, however, must have caused even the most hardened, *outre Face*-reading style gurus to blink – and hardened hacks to guffaw a 'Christ almighty, cop a load of that!' Charlie had always had a liking for leather and had even designed some of his own outfits. This one, however, looked like it had been designed by a recently redundant member of the *Blake's Seven* props department. Words can barely do it justice but here goes. The jacket was a low-buttoned affair, the lapels eventually criss-crossing somewhere just south of Charlie's navel. The trousers, closely hugging Charlie's impressive thighs, made his lower half seem in still shots, look like something from World of Leather's January sale. To top all this off, he was clutching a handbag. A little leather, pouchy handbag. Lord knows what was in it. Gathered hacks and photographers must all have been inclined to exclaim, in unison, like Aunt Augusta in *The Importance of Being Earnest*: 'A handbag??'

Of course, the hacks would quickly have swallowed any indignation they harboured at the fashion excesses of the younger generation. The uppermost thought was, 'Blimey, we've got a right one here. We can have some sport with this geezer. Please God, let him sign to a London club!'

That decision would be deferred until after the British Championships at the end of the month, with Charlie down in the squad and due to make his first appearance at Wembley. Jock Stein invoking merely the authority of his own, formidable will, brusquely called a moratorium on any transfer manoeuvrings towards Charlie. 'No one will now be speaking to the player until after the Wembley game,' he decreed austerely.

If Stein's intention was to focus Charlie on the task in hand, he hadn't succeeded. England tonked Scotland 2-0, and Charlie froze under the floodlit Wembley glare. Dogs had run on to the famous Wembley turf in past years that had contributed more to the game than Charlie did that night. He knew only too well he'd screwed up. 'I felt like a wee boy among grown men,' he confessed poignantly later, adding that the stress of his impending transfer had inhibited his performance.

Liverpool were still in the running, but Bob Paisley seemed less inclined to do the legwork than the new favourites in the bid for Charlie – Arsenal. Though not before Gunter Netzer's Hamburg threw their hat into the ring at the last minute. Arsenal had been sniffing around for a replacement for Lee Chapman, whom they'd signed from Stoke and had proved a disaster. Charlie, Terry Neill and Don Howe would thrash things out at a Park Lane Hotel – but Bev Walker had also arranged a preliminary meeting at, of all places, a pre-election televised Conservative youth rally.

'Scottish people could forgive Charlie a lot, but not this,' comments one Scottish journalist and friend of Charlie Nicholas drily. As news filtered back to Glasgow that Charlie hadn't just shared a Tory platform but had also chatted amiably for a few moments with the loathsome gorgon Thatcher, bitterness was in grave danger of intensifying. Charlie's father, Chic, a print union official, remarked reservedly that he was 'surprised' to see Charlie up there with . . . her. Bev Walker moved to oil things over, assuring everyone that Charlie had not been up there to endorse Conservative politics – indeed, he wasn't able to vote at all as the election would take place while he was away on tour with Scotland in Canada and had failed to register for a postal vote. Still, that begged the question, what on earth was he doing up there at all? Anything to oblige . . .

Years later, Charlie would offer his own explanation. 'It was my old agent who arranged that. He was obviously a Tory. I'm not particularly knowledgeable about politics but my family have always voted Labour and that's the way I'd vote. But, coming down from London that day, all I knew was that I was doing some publicity thing. Even when we came to the hall, I didn't know what it was. The first thing I knew is when I got called out on to the stage. I couldn't believe it when Margaret Thatcher walked in! I was embarrassed about it afterwards.'

Meanwhile, Jock Stein had satisfied himself in his own mind as to the reason for Charlie's poor showing against England. Poor awareness in front of goal? Inadequate concentration? Failure to adapt to different tactics? No – it was that gold earring. Jock Stein ordered him to remove it, prior to Scotland's upcoming three-day tour of Canada. From that earring, he surmised, emanated all the decadence that was rotting away at Charlie's form. Furthermore, he ordered him to ditch the outlandish leather suits and, when with the squad, adhere to regulation team jacket and slacks. Charlie complied. Anything to oblige.

The three-day tour of Canada would provide another hiatus in the transfer circus. 'At least there won't be any agents floating about out there,' snorted Jock Stein. By now, however, Charlie's mind was made up. On June 10, it was official. Charlie would be joining Arsenal for £650,000.

Billy McNeill had tried to the last to persuade him to give Celtic at least a couple more years. He'd offered him the best possible package he could. His repeated fulsome songs of praise to his talent had reassured Charlie of the high regard he held him in. Charlie's own family hadn't entirely been able to conceal their misgivings about a move down to London for Charlie. 'I'm a wee bit upset about him going to London,' confessed Rena, his mother, to *Woman* magazine. 'I've got a bit of a worry that he might fall into the wrong company.' Celtic fans were distraught. How could Charlie, an avowed true Celt, turn his back on his ain folk for the English shilling?

How indeed? At Arsenal, Charlie would be on a package that would see him earn a basic of £2,000 a week. They'd just about managed to outbid Man Utd, who had been offering him £100,000 a year. The Celtic board had conferred and authorised Billy McNeill to make the most generous counter-offer they felt they could manage to retain the services of their young superstar.

£400 per week.

Charlie later described Celtic's offer as an 'incitement to leave'.

Says then team-mate Danny Crainie, 'We were all supporters of Celtic as kids and they played on that fact. We never got financially rewarded because we were just happy to play for the club. Who could blame Charlie for leaving? It's okay talking about loyalty but loyalty has to come from both sides.'

Only months later, Billy McNeill left Celtic himself. The reasons were varied but ultimately they came down to one thing. Money. Or the lack of it. The Celtic board's parsimonious, blinkered vision would bring crisis upon their heads in years to come. In the meantime, they were content to wave bye-bye to Charlie as he set off on his way to Highbury . . .

Chapter Six

Charlie's decision to move to Highbury in 1983 was considered a surprise one by those in the know. All the smart money had been on him going to Liverpool, a bigger, altogether more cultured outfit, whose combination of systematic and stylish play would seem to have been the perfect place to bring on the brilliant but still youthful tearaway to loftier heights of sophistication.

No one could quite envisage Charlie working with Arsenal coach Don Howe, a man whose reputation was for bread and butter, better-safe-than-sorry, defensive tactics, with maybe some attacking flair later if you were lucky, didn't seem entirely Charlie-friendly. Bev Walker, however, was quick to reassure, 'Some people are a bit worried about Don Howe's reputation and so was Charlie. But Howe made it clear that Charlie wouldn't be expected to keep dropping back. He's at Arsenal to do what he does best – score goals.'

Others, however, suspected that the real reason Charlie had gone to London was so that he could spend as much time as possible with his burgeoning commercial interests. Bev Walker had set up for him a private company, Charlie Nicholas (Scotland) Ltd, and had already got him a series of endorsements, including Nike football boots; Burtons, whose autumn fashion range was imminent; promoting a range of cars; and lending his name to a column in the *Sun*. He and Charlie made no secret of their intention that, by the time he was 25, Charlie should be a millionaire.

Jock Stein, who was earlier so solicitous in his avuncular guidance to Charlie in the matter of leisurewear, was presumably hoping to be similarly helpful when he bluntly informed the press that in his view, Charlie had made a big mistake going to Highbury. 'My view is that if Charlie was considering only his football career then Liverpool was the place to go. Of course,' he added satirically, 'if commercial interests are uppermost in Charlie's mind then Arsenal is the place to go.'

As Charlie rode into town, there were many who secretly nurtured the wish that he was riding for a fall. When you are showered in obscene abundance with youth, talent, wealth and sex appeal, it's not always easy to find well-wishers. The *Daily Mail* proffered the opinion that he might be swayed by the 'bright lights' of London. The *Daily Mirror*, wondered if he might find London's bright lights too much of a temptation. The *Daily Express* declared that Charlie could well find that the bright lights of the capital city too hard to resist.

Charlie was aware of his reputation as a playboy and, while not entirely disowning it, assured us that he was just a regular lad who liked a night out. 'I enjoy a few drinks on a Saturday night after the game. I like going to discos. Why shouldn't I? I'm not married, I'm young and I enjoy life.

'But that's on a Saturday AFTER a match. Before a game it's different. Thursdays and Friday nights don't exist for me.'

One journalist would later report having sat with Charlie as he quaffed several glasses of Bucks Fizz hours before a match. But that was still to come.

Charlie arrived at Highbury for his first day with the club amid the flashing of bubbles and a scramble of journalists, wearing his now-familiar combination of leather trousers and no socks, and accompanied as ever by Bev Walker. Bob Wilson, President of the Supporters' Club was there to greet him – as was a cardboard cut out of Roy of the Rovers, transported to the scene in the back of a car. The hero of the eponymous soccer magazine frequently insulted the intelligence of his young but not entirely dim readership by turning up at momentous footballing events such as this, posing for photos with the celebrities concerned. Charlie accepted cardboard Roy's hearty greetings. Anything to oblige. On occasions such as this he must have felt pretty two-dimensional too.

The fans were mad for Charlie. Within hours of the news breaking that he was signing for the club, hundreds of season ticket enquiries had been handled. It was one in the eye for their north London rivals Spurs, the more to be savoured because Charlie had actually rejected overtures from White Lane. He'd picked us! The fans felt like wallflowers at the town hall dance chosen for a waltz by the beau of the county. Gooners walked tall. Nick Hornby was so fired up with inspiration at Charlie's arrival that he resolved to become a writer.

Spurs had had the better of things in recent years – they'd won the FA Cup for two years on the trot, thanks to the crowd-pleasing, electrifying football of the likes of Ossie Ardiles, Ricky Villa, Glenn Hoddle and Garth Crooks. Spurs were a multicultural, exotic melting pot of continental flair, pulse-quickening pace and elegance on the ball. Arsenal, meanwhile, had Brian Talbot. Arsenal had to eat up the reverence of neutrals for White Hart Lane, cathedral of footballing elegance, and the implication underlying all those commentator's effusions that it was always a sin against proper football whenever Spurs lost, that a Spurs defeat meant a triumph for mediocrity and greyness.

Arsenal, meanwhile, were boring, boring Arsenal, ugly, graceless, churlish, joyless and scoreless, until about 20 minutes to go, after which they sat unbudgingly on their lead. Sure, only a few years earlier, they'd been involved in the most exciting FA Cup final since the Matthews final of 1953 when, moments after Manchester United's Sammy McIlroy had ushered the ball through a scrum of Arsenal defenders to level the scores at 2-2, a white-booted, elfin Liam Brady scampered one last time up the left, setting up the cross for Alan Sunderland to make it 3-2 only a minute later and with just a minute to go. But then, of course, both Brady and fellow talented frontman Frank Stapleton had been allowed by Arsenal to head for the glory fields of Juventus and Man U respectively.

Many supporters found it hard to forgive Arsenal. Remembers Nick Hornby, 'We were desperately short of heroes at that time. The worst thing about Brady and Stapleton leaving is that it was pretty obvious that they didn't do so with any reluctance

– they'd wanted to go. It reflected badly on the team and made us feel bad about ourselves.'

Years later, Charlie divulged the real reason why he had gone to Arsenal. He had heard, on excellent authority, that Liam Brady, now playing his football in Italy, had been all set to rejoin Arsenal in a sensational swoop the day after Charlie was due to sign up. The prospect of forming a partnership upfront with the Republic of Ireland genius, a hero among Celts, was too much to resist. However, at the very last minute, the deal, it seems, fell through, by which time Charlie was a Gooner.

Charlie had been drafted in not just in the hope of fulfilling this need for heroes but also to boost attendances, which had been in steady decline, with Arsenal finishing an unthinkable tenth in the First Division the season before, their worst performance since the mid-seventies, when the Gunners' idea of a glamour player was Terry 'same name as Henry' Mancini. Arsenal were in danger of slithering out of football's Top Five, of degenerating into some sort of southern Coventry. They'd tried before – they'd actually paid £1 million for QPR's Clive Allen, only to exchange him almost immediately for Kenny Samson, before he'd even kicked a football in an Arsenal shirt in anger. Then there'd been Lee Chapman, about whom the less said the better. Now they had Charlie and the prospect of goals galore. He'd scored over 50 for Celtic, that would be just the start. He could do the same for Arsenal. Fifty goals. Or 60, even 70 in a year or so's time, maybe, when he settled in a bit. Let's not pressurise the lad. Bob Wilson, the monotonous voice of reason at Arsenal, tried to cool the fever of expectation, saying that if

Charlie could score 20 goals in his first season that'd be really something – but hopes ran high all the same.

Fellow professionals weighed in with their advices. Said Bobby Moore, 'Everything in moderation. Do the best you can do and keep your feet on the ground.' (That advice Charlie always followed – he never was much cop at headers.) Bobby Charlton warned, 'Work hard, get lots of sleep and if you must drink, make it beer.'

There were sanguine predictions for Charlie's fortunes off the field too. Astrologer Russell Grant was commissioned by one of the less highbrow papers to assess the stars of the star. His conclusions made for portentous reading. 'He's like Frank Bough,' wrote Grant. 'A Capricorn with Sagittarius rising.' He also predicted a fair wind for his business ventures, thanks to 'Saturn's conjunction with Sagittarius'. Charlie's sex life too was smiled upon by the alignments of the cosmos – 'As a Capricorn with Venus he could give James Bond a run for his money.'

Charlie's early days at Highbury were filled with nonsense like this. In his first few months at the club he didn't get a single day off, what with rushing off to endorse this, pose for so-and-so, appear on such-and-such. Fashion spread after fashion spread appeared in the middle of the pops – Charlie bare-chested, Charlie sporting a thick gold chain, Charlie in 'gangster style' cream suit and trilby ('Jacket £29.99, trousers £16.99, shirt £5.50 – all from Top Man!'), Charlie in his latest customized suede and leather concoction, Charlie looking on the point of tears in intimate thigh-hugging bermuda shorts, even Charlie in his underwear. Anything to oblige.

His first footballing engagement was a close season tour of West Germany in which, against Teutonic minnows Bochum, he was clattered to the ground and was taken off injured at half time. It was then that Terry Neill introduced him to a recent invention – shinpads. Amazingly, in several seasons of being booted up and down the most hostile and forbidding pitches of the Scotland, Charlie Nicholas had never worn shinpads. He would have to now, or face disciplinary action.

Come the day of Charlie's Arsenal début proper, high expectation was laced with a tinge of uncertainty. There had been reports that in pre-season matches, Charlie had been deliberately starved of the ball, running into space then throwing up his arms in despair when the ball never reached. *Au contraire*, said Charlie. Jealous team mates? Never. The worst he had had to endure from them was a volley of bad Russ Abbott Scotsman impersonations every time he entered the dressing room. Footballers like a laugh.

Charlie did his best to play down the hype surrounding him. 'I have been over-publicised. I'm as sick of seeing my face in the papers as I'm sure the fans are. I honestly don't think I'm as good as everyone is making out.' What's more, aiding and abetting the hype was beginning to fatigue him.

The first match of Arsenal's season was a home fixture against Luton, who went on to upset Arsenal in the 1988 Cup Final, but Arsenal usually took the points off them without too much of a fight.

Before the game, in the tunnel, a bout of nerves passed

through Charlie like a dose of laxative. It was natural. Graham Rix reassured him with a 'Right, man! Let's go!' But the officials insisted that Charlie hang back as he was to be introduced separately. Charlie felt a proper Charlie. But he emerged, boosted and bashful to an ebullient welcome from a packed terrace of fans, most of whom were sporting Charlie Nicholas hairdos and even Charlie Nicholas gold earrings. The club had even appointed a DJ, in the new 'with-it' spirit engendered by Charlie. Hitherto, the only time Arsenal's world had bissected with that of disc jockeydom was when Radio Two's Pete Murray declared himself a Gunner.

It turned out to be a solid but unspectacular performance, a 2-1 victory with goals from Woodcock and McDermott. Charlie modestly did his bit, making intelligent runs of the ball, quick-silver darts into space and twinking into life with a couple of touches which raised yelps of delight. He went off to a perhaps over-generous standing ovation. The *Sunday Times* gave an effusive notice: 'Though a single game is scant evidence, it can be said with some confidence that Charlie Nicholas will prosper in England.' Others were less certain, accusing him of 'trying too hard', not a charge that would often be levelled at Charlie in later years, and 'dropping back too often and too deep.'

The next fixture against Wolves at Molineux was a more qualified success as Charlie scored both goals, one a handily converted penalty, the other when he got on the end of a long ball from David O'Leary. Two games, two goals, so far, so good.

Then, the first mini-crisis of the season – Arsenal lost three games on the trot.

Charlie seemed to be living up to his new resolve to cut out some of the sillier photo stunts when he failed to turn up for a picture session involving himself and 'The Exhibitionists', five leggy, beshorted gels who kicked footballs about for the benefit of a tabloid photographer with a Diana Ross-like eye for goal. His scoutlike abstemiousness didn't help as the Gunners went down 1-0 to the Saints in front of a near-capacity crowd at the Dell, attracted by the allure of Charlie.

Defeat followed against Man Utd, 3-2, with Charlie unable to make the difference. Then came Liverpool and an early chance, as a move involving Paul Davis and Graham Rix finally reached Nicholas, a neatly weighted ball which he brought down on his chest before volleying sweetly, past the helpless Grobbelaar – the crowd gasped, filled their lungs ready for the roar that would green Charlie's first home goal – but the ball crashed against the woodwork and a terraceful of chests sagged in dismay. After that, Liverpool kept a weather-eye on Charlie and, one exquisite dummy apart, he was frozen out of the game. 'He's still learning his trade,' explained Terry Neill patiently afterwards – and the critics laid off for the time being, some blaming Tony Woodcock for not being Frank Stapleton.

This left Arsenal perilously low in the table, lower even than Birmingham City. Nothing was quite going right for Charlie. Having assured *Sun* readers via his regular column that if they thought he was going to be partying down London's swankiest clubs every night they were very much mistaken, he was ambushed by TV cameras just as he walked into Stringfellows with Suzanne Dando on his arm. Dando, a former gymnast was one of the fit and sporty women in Bev Walker's agency and a future shining star of regional panto, one of the first of a string of semi-celebrity females who would be snapped hanging on Charlie's arm. Embarrassed, Charlie and Suzanne fled into the night. A few days later, they were involved in a crash as Charlie swerved to avoid an oncoming vehicle. No one was hurt but the vehicle was a write-off.

After all this, Charlie could have done with a nice, relaxing weekend – which fortunately was just what Arsenal had, in the form of a fixture against Notts County. Arsenal made a 4-0 turkey-shoot of that one. Woodcock scored. Rix scored. Charlie didn't. Next up were Norwich, at home, more easy meat, surely. 3-0. McDermott racked up two. Even Lee Chapman got on the scoresheet, just to show what sort of yeastily benevolent mood Norwich were in. But Charlie? Charlie picked up a knock and limped off after 72 minutes. The fans kept faith in him, with rapturous applause. They were patient, especially when they learned that the injury Charlie had picked up in that pre-season warmup match in Germany had inhibited his training. Well there you are, they assured one another.

Against QPR, however, Arsenal got back to losing ways, going down 2-0 and the sweet taste of irony for Rangers' Clive Allen, whom Arsenal had bought and then sold immediately. This was followed by defeat at Coventry 1-0, after which Terry Neill showed distinct sings of disquiet. 'Charlie just didn't play well,' he commented numbly at the press conference afterwards. 'I don't know, I don't know . . .' he added, his voice trailing away down a stream of troubled waters.

Charlie's confidence beginning to ebb; still shaken by that car crash, troubled by the lingeringly dodgy state of his ligaments, and beginning to blink under the glare of those much-vaunted bright lights, Charlie was in a delicate psychological condition. What he needed was a gentle whisper of encouragement, a geeing up from some footballing father who'd seen success and failure and learned to treat those impostors just the same, a kind word, for his flagging ego to be kneaded and massaged back into shape.

What he got was a hefty boot up the backside from the burly, surly Jock Stein. Charlie had retained his place in the Scotland squad, having redeemed his rabbit-in-the-headlights performance against England with a brilliant solo goal in a 3-0 victory against Canada. But the sceptical Stein still made it quite clear to Charlie that he was in the squad if not quite under sufferance then certainly on probation. He barked at him like a Sergeant Major in training – and, a day or so before their big European fixture against Belgium, issued this stern injunction: 'He may have cost three quarter of a million pounds and he may have had a brilliant half hour against Switzerland. But he has not set the heather on fire at Arsenal and he has not done it for us since that Swiss game.'

Charlie didn't find this sort of heavy-handed chivvying particularly helpful as his nerves were under enough strain already. 'It's not very nice to know that at 21 you could be about to play your last game for Scotland,' he complained. In the event it was Charlie's goal that saved Scotland that night at Hampden, earning them a 1-1 draw. Not that even this was enough for Stein: 'I still feel he has a hit to go at this level.' And, just in case Fate felt it had been too kind of Charlie of late, he would arrive home from the Scotland international to discover that some bastard had burgled his house.

There was to be no quick upturn in Charlie's fortunes. Arsenal played Nottingham Forest at home and won 4-1, but no thanks to Charlie, who was taken off. 'It had nothing to do with injuries,' said Terry Neill, pointedly. 'We just needed more goals.'

The papers were beginning to show their exasperation. 'One pass,' snorted one report. 'One pass. That was all he did. In front of goal, he was invisible.'

Don Howe decided that it was time to engage in some subtle reverse psychology. He publicly urged Charlie Nicholas to 'belt up' and stop discussing his career publicly (difficult when he had a weekly column in the *Sun* to fill) and let others take the strain of spokesmanship.

Nicholas had admitted that he was beginning to panic about his goal drought. Howe made a cack-handed attempt to put things in some sort of perspective: 'Charlie must remember he's done nothing in his career if you compare him with someone like our Tony Woodcock, who has played in European Cups and in World Cups and has been a top star in West Germany.' Having thus assured Charlie that he was an over-valued nonentity, Howe concluded, 'So he shouldn't pile the pressure on himself unnecessarily.' Thank you, Don.

The Aston Villa away fixture would provide another unlikely goalfest in what was proving rather an unsettled, topsy-turvy season. Arsenal buried Villa with a six-goal salute, with goals from Woodcock! Woodcock! Woodcock! Woodcock! And finally – Woodcock! But no Charlie. Once more, he hit the bar.

A twenty-year-old Charlie Nicholas at Celtic
– 'The most exciting player I have ever seen,' said manager Billy McNeill

Pulling the trigger against Aberdeen. In the 1982/83
season he would amass an astonishing fifty-one goals

All hail Arsenal's
'King Charlie'
– but would the
crown fit?

Ups and downs in his first season. Charlie scores from the spot against Wolves ...

... then is denied by West Ham's Phil Parkes.
'Charlie is shooting blanks!' crows the press

In action for his country during the 1986 World Cup

Carted off injured against Denmark. Scotland too would retire early from the competition

An eighties fashion victim through and through. Check the shiny strides!

An increasingly rare moment of triumph, against Southampton, 1986

Forced smiles as Charlie welcomes George Graham to Arsenal
– they wouldn't last

Spurs's Richard Gough meets cheeky Charlie, 1987

At last! Charlie nudges home the first of two goals
against Liverpool in the 1987 Littlewoods Cup Final

'Sell Me If You Dare!' An exultant Charlie challenges
George Graham after triumph against Liverpool

What was the matter? Why couldn't he hack it? Was it just some sort of mental block? Was he spending too much time carousing? Was energy spent on commercial ventures eating into his form? Was energy spent on Suzanne Dando eating into his lust for goals?

The *Sunday Times*, in a feature entitled 'The Gunner Without Ammo', suggested that the Arsenal formation wasn't suiting Charlie. In a game against Plymouth, the feature pointed out, he'd spent much of his time upfront in the wilderness, detached and frustrated, a forlorn and lonely figure waiting for passes that never came.

'At Celtic, Charlie Nicholas flourished because of their fast-passing and attacking style. The midfield were very quick to get forward and support attacks. At Arsenal, the midfield are wary of pushing up. Nicholas, a one- or two-touch players is given too much to do on the ball, making him a likelier captive for tight markers.'

Don Howe was having none of this. 'His reaction to losing the ball is bad,' he snapped. 'He should work harder to get it back.'

Elsewhere, the ghost of Peter Marinello was invoked. He had always been considered the seventies prototype for Charlie. A fashion victim in the early seventies, all flock wallpaper shirts and cravats as wide as airport runways, he had come down to Arsenal from Hibernian with the sign 'Highland George Best' hanging around his neck, for a then colossal £100,000. In three and a half seasons, however, he played only 32 times and scored just three goals. His concentration, they reckoned, had been affected by the alternative lifestyle that beckoned as a heart-throb and denizen of the 'discotheques' and 'swinging boutiques'. He plummeted to Portsmouth, then Fulham, then Motherwell, then an Edinburgh pub. In an article reeking with *schadenfreude* he expressed his fears that Charlie would go the same way as he did.

Whether it was the thought of ending up running a pub in Edinburgh or whether the ball finally ran his way, Charlie finally broke his long drought with a goal against Spurs at White Hart Lane in November 1983. It was significant that he should come good against Arsenal's fiercest rivals, indicating a latent, instinctive sense of drama and the big occasion. But this was only the League Cup. In the First Division, still no joy. And now the club hit a wretched spell, with four defeats on the trot. 0-3 at Leicester. 1-2 defeat at the hands of third division Walsall with all Arsenal ears burning with the ringing guffaws of the football world. 0-1 against WBA, with Charlie, now caught in that desperate psychological syndrome where the more desperate you are to score, the more howlingly you miss the sitter, blazing over the bar and mis-kicking twice in front of goal. 'Nicholas looked a wretched sight,' noted one reporter, 'pottering about as if he'd been pulled off Hackney Marshes at the last minute.' Yet it wasn't for Charlie's blood that the crowd bayed. Finally, after a 1-3 away defeat at West Ham, Peter Hill-Wood acceded to the chants of demonstrating fans and sacked his 'friend of 20 years' Terry Neill.

Charlie by now was so frustrated he'd taken to going out on to the golf course alone and thwacking balls about at random to give vent to his energy. Then, in the next home game, victory!

Against Watford! A hat-trick! Unfortunately it was for young Raphael Meade. All that Charlie got on the end of was an upending, bonecrunching tackle from Watford's Price.

By Boxing Day, with still just two First Division goals to his credit, Charlie must have been wondering about installing standpipes in the opposition goal. But Arsenal were back at Spurs and, would you believe it, he scored not one but two Christmas crackers. The first looked to be yet another mis-hit – but as the ball cannoned back off the Spurs defender, Charlie was quickest to lapse on to it and, without seeming to have either the purchase or the leverage, hoiked it over the keeper into the net from 25 yards out with his left peg. The second was a lob-in over the stranded keeper as Charlie latched on to a long ball through the middle. So simple, so elegant, what could the problem have been? Perhaps Charlie didn't just score goals against any old riff-raff but deliberately held back for the special team, the special day. 'The bigger the game,' Charlie once said, 'the more I feel.'

He'd still to do it at home, though. That was the curse, the gremlin, he really had to dispel. He got his chance the next week against Birmingham. A penalty, in the 77th minute with Arsenal a goal down. As he picked up the ball and gathered himself to take the conversion, you could have heard a pin drop. As he trotted up and slotted a right-footer into the back of the net you'd have been lucky to have heard a bomb drop. The pandemonium that heralded this goal, a mere equaliser against Birmingham, at home, hadn't even been matched for writhing volume when Arsenal clinched the double.

Chapter Seven

With the removal of Terry Neill, the choice among fans for new Arsenal manager was, according to the polls, Malcolm McDonald. Such times. How wise a decision that would have proved we shall never know, though we could probably hazard a decent guess. The man they got was Don Howe, coach at the club for the past 14 years and now finally promoted. Though Don Howe had spent years at the highest managerial level, both national and international, he never really rose very much above the level of figure of fun in the eyes of many. Maybe it was that pork pie hat, maybe it was that West Midlands accent and the fact that whenever he spoke you couldn't help but be reminded of the geezer in *It Ain't Half Hot Mum* who always spat out his food as he talked. He never had the sort of charisma or go-ahead outlook to bring the crowds flocking back – during his tenure, attendances at Highbury dropped at times to below 20,000. Chant 'Boring, boring Arsenal' and somehow it was the image of Howe that flickered to mind. He was, however, respected by players as a coach. And his first move, in addressing the Nicholas question was to do exactly what he'd promised Charlie he wouldn't do – drop him back to midfield.

The experiment initially proved a resounding failure and much wonderment at what the hell Howe was playing at. Players generally moved back a line as age caught up with them and their legs began to go. Charlie had only just turned 22 and, having reported ditched Suzanne Dando and been seen in the company of Prince Andrew's former girlfriend Carolyn Seaward, there was evidently life in the young dog yet.

As Arsenal crashed out of the FA Cup 3-2 to Middlesbrough, Charlie looked distinctly uncomfortable in his new role. He seemed to have been shoved back to make room for the ebullient Paul Mariner, an uncomplicated but effective centre forward, who began knocking them in in lieu of Charlie.

Charlie didn't seem to know quite what to do with himself – he was, as the always orotund Brian Glanville put it, 'Neither upfield fish nor midfield fowl.' Arsenal started to put together the sort of results that would eventually drag them back up to sixth place – but Charlie wasn't at the centre of the festivities. Even in a 4-1 victory against Ipswich Charlie was described, again by Brian Glanville as cutting an 'almost pathetic figure'. 'The best course Nicholas should follow,' he surmised, 'is surely to go back to Scotland and rebuild his reputation as other Scots such as Auld, Bannon and McGarvey have done in the past.'

There was no way back into the Scottish team for Charlie as Jock Stein announced, with almost grim satisfaction, that Charlie wouldn't be in the squad to face Wales in their upcoming home championship tie. 'This time last year we were opti-mistic about Nicholas but he hasn't even been playing upfront recently.'

As question marks began to pop up everywhere as to whether Charlie was in the right place and whether he'd done the right thing, attention turned towards Bev Walker, suspected by many of running his young protégé into the ground. He held up his hands in denial. 'I would have preferred Charlie to have gone to Italy,' he claimed.

Terry MacNeill, writing in the *News of the World*, also doubted whether Charlie was at all cut out for the hurly burly of the English First Division. 'Charlie doesn't get into the six-yard box too many times in 90 minutes. The old sweats marking him don't mind him looking pretty on the ball in areas where he can't do any damage.

'The North Bank at Highbury won't hear a word against him and it's premature and potty to write him off. Yet unless there's a significant improvement and a more identifiable role for the misfit, there must be a temptation to sell him.

'Arsenal gambled with Charlie because they wanted to change their image. They yearned to be loved as well as respected. Which was understandable with everyone chuntering on about entertaining.

'But maybe Arsenal should have true to their traditions – bloody minded, organised and hard to beat. They might be better off flogging Charlie, getting back to their roots and leaving the entertaining to West Ham and Spurs.'

Gradually, however, Charlie began to creep back to something like respectable form. He scored against Wolves and Stoke as the green shoots of spring emerged. And then, uncannily, once more against Spurs, he pulled another rabbit out of the hat with his best performance all season. In what was described as a 'nervous and brutish' encounter, in which Arsenal emerged 3-2 victors, Charlie manufactured a goal reminiscent of his vintage Celtic best. Hanging back slightly deep, Charlie watched from afar developments in the Spurs penalty box as a cross came in and Mariner, temporarily nonplussed, headed back in the vague direction of his own goal. Charlie seized on the stray ball and, letting instinct take over, spirited his way through a seemingly impenetrable thicket of Spurs defenders, did a quick one-two, took the ball out wide past the flailing keeper and then, with almost sarcastic consideredness, placed the ball in at the far post with the cool acumen of a snooker maestro.

He was also involved in the fast-moving build up that led to Woodcock's goal, a simple flick-on creating acres for his partner to run into where before there had been only yards. Catching this footage in isolation, marvel at the fluency, the swashing, the buckling, the musketeer arrogance and you'd wonder what all the alarm and despondency was about. Small wonder that the only other thing he did of note the rest of that season was pick up a rare sending off after a bit of a tear-up with Andy Peake. With this performance, Charlie renewed on his goodwill for next year.

Strictly speaking, however, Charlie's haul of just 12 goals in all competitions for the season had to rank as a pretty inauspicious start. A bit of a disaster, even. Which is why many welcomed Charlie's decision to drop agent Bev Walker in May of

1984. Walker had already been under scrutiny for alleged under-the-counter payments to Olympic gold medal-winning decathlete Daly Thompson and judo star Neil Adams, compromising their amateur status. Now it was claimed that he had picked up more than £13,000 from Arsenal for negotiating Charlie's transfer from Celtic to Arsenal – with a further £23,000 to follow. Walker had also reneged on commissions due to Brian Jacks and money owed to Suzanne Dando for endorsement work she'd carried out – and now, his little sports empire was collapsing about his ears.

With Walker out of his hair, surely Charlie could create a fresh start, ditch some of the more distracting commercial commitments, kick all that Champagne Charlie nonsense into touch. He now entrusted his affairs to fellow Scot and agent/minder Frank Boyd.

But things didn't get much better. Time after time, in interview after interview, Charlie would patiently explain that he was no playboy souse. 'Everything I do seems to get exaggerated. If I go into a bar and have a lager shandy, the word goes round that I'm knocking back the bottles of champagne. By the time it gets back to the papers or my manager at Arsenal, I'm lying in the gutter!'

It didn't help Charlie to maintain this line, however, when he was hauled up for the second time in three years for a drink-driving offence. Back up in Glasgow in late May to visit friends, he had been spotted by a keen-eyed citizen driving erratically and the police were alerted to the zig-zag progress of his car as it approached the lights. According to prosecutor, Alistair

MacSporran (laughter in court), Charlie had been breathalysed and had tested positive. The defence put as pious a slant as they could on Charlie's misdemeanour. 'Mr Nicholas had been visiting friends and neighbours. In the subsequent course of visiting friends and neighbours he partook of their hospitality, which he now knew he should have declined.' The judge nodded sympathetically and banned Charlie from driving for three years.

There had also been a rather absurd skirmish involving the alleged stealing of a chip – yes, a chip – from a couple while holidaying in Ibiza, but that was nothing. Nonsense. The couple posed fetchingly for agency shots displaying the boyfriend's busted ribs, but the whole thing seemed destined to blow over.

There was further adversity when Charlie returned back up to Celtic for a testimonial match with Arsenal, when he was barracked, jeered and abused by the Jungle end. They still hadn't forgiven him for 'abandoning his roots', as one cab driver growled – and, though he did receive a warmer reception from others in the main stand, the pang of having been rejected by the fans with whom he'd not just felt such a rapport but once been part of, was sharp indeed. Ironically, Kenny Dalglish, who had put in seven solid years of faithful and fruitful service to Celtic before finally leaving for Liverpool had received a far worse reception, a terrible roasting when he'd returned to Parkhead just a year later. However, by 1985 when Dalglish led a Liverpool team up to Celtic after the Heysel disaster, all had long been forgiven.

Interest still lingered in Charlie's private life. He'd reportedly turned down £10,000 from the *News of the World* to talk about his personal life and drinking habits. Perhaps he reconsidered, more likely he was stitched up. Whatever, in November, an article beneath the eloquent banner 'BIRDS, BOOZE AND ME – by Charlie Nicholas'.

The accompanying photo had Charlie looking uncannily like his hero Bono of U2, sitting cross-legged in a loose-fitting white tracksuit, drinking tea, akin to a member of some obscure Eastern sect devoted to temperance and meditation. There was nothing especially ascetic about the accompanying text in which Charlie, protesting once again that his playboy image was a myth, seemed to be digging himself deeper into the mire. 'I don't drink like a fish,' he said. 'I have the odd glass of champagne and orange juice and I never touch spirits. On a boys' night out after a game the most I'll have is seven or eight pints of lager. To me, that isn't being drunk.'

Having thus assured us of his near-teetotal status, Charlie went on to stress the ordinariness of his sexual life. He was just a normal young man, he urged, whose dalliances were pretty much the average sort of thing for anyone his age. 'When you're 22, fit and with the normal appetites it's impossible to stay celibate,' he explained. Whereupon he went on to give a racy synopsis of his flings with Suzanne Dando ('She's a lovely girl but when we were out she wanted pictures of us taken together. I didn't.'), Janis Lee Burns, the girl in the Cadbury's flake advert who'd recently had a brush with John McEnroe ('I just call her the Flake and if you pardon the pun, she's very tasty.') and former Miss UK Carolyn Seaward ('I'm not too proud to admit a failure there.') Currently footloose, he dreamt aloud of settling down with some nice, steady, homespun girl and sharing with her his new luxury flat whose fixtures and fittings included a mirrored ceiling in the bedroom.

All in all then, Charlie seemed satisfied, pretty much the usual common-or-garden, boy-next-door stuff. The editor of the *News of the World* was certainly well satisfied.

By stark contrast, around the same time, Charlie was interviewed by the then almost painfully right-on rock weekly, *New Musical Express*. This actually made perfect sense. The rise to prominence of Charlie Nicholas coincided not just with the rise of U2 but also of a whole explosion of post-punk Scottish groups in the early eighties. There was Orange Juice, from Alan Horne's prolific Postcard label. Simple Minds. The Blue Nile. The Cocteau Twins. The Associates, whose lead singer, the late Billy Mackenzie, in many ways resembled Charlie in spirit even more than Bono, with his flamboyant, pyrotechnic sense of drama. 'What was always great to me about Charlie,' said James Payne, former contributor to *Not The View*, the Celtic fanzine, 'is that whenever he was interviewed by *Shoot* or one of those magazines and they asked him about his favourite bands, he didn't come out with the usual stuff footballers came out with – Lionel Ritchie, Rod Stewart – he talked about The Sex Pistols and The Clash.'

Indeed, for the *NME* interview, Charlie listed his favourite bands as 'U2, The Alarm, Sade, The Psychedelic Furs, Depeche Mode'. One or two duffers in there but for 1984 that was quite a staggeringly hip selection. Pat Nevin, too, one time team mate at Celtic Boys' Club and another attacking Scot who would cut a dash in the English league had already been noted for the left-field nature of his music tastes. He was the first ever footballer either side of the border to dress and comport himself like a member of Joy Division. But whereas Nevin was more the student of this new music, Nicholas was more the existential embodiment of this brash, confident new spirit. Nicholas probably didn't see the music as anything much more than a lifestyle accoutrement. But he and Nevin represented a generation who nurtured both a passion for indie music and a passion for soccer, and found that the two were not necessarily incompatible.

In these days when it's practically mandatory for squad members of Liverpool and Man Utd under 25 to be present at all gigs by Blur, Oasis and Pulp and date at least one Spice Girl, it's easy to forget how far apart the two cultures of music press rock and football once were. In their own ways Pat Nevin and Charlie Nicholas were groundbreakers, wittingly or otherwise. For with indie rock came an indie rock sensibility, sceptical and acerbic, which informed the tone of music fanzines. The next logical step was to bring that sensibility to football – hence the likes of *When Saturday Comes* and the first wave of football fanzines, which would seen develop a crucial role as the consciences (and irreverent thorns in the side) of the clubs, forcing issues that had hitherto simply been neglected.

All of that down to Charlie Nicholas and his dodgy haircuts. Improbable, yet true.

The *NME* piece was a sympathetic, even adulatory one, with Charlie taking the opportunity once again to give the lie to the notion that he was a champagne guzzling, womanising nightcrawler. 'Sometimes I am a bit of a wind-up. A few days ago a reporter from the national press came up and said he'd heard a rumour that my manager had fined me £1000 for being drunk in some club.

'Things like that really get on my nerves. So I either just laugh or wind the person up by saying something like "Yeah, that's right". I'm probably better off just keeping my mouth shut but sometimes I just can't resist the wind-up.'

However, when the *NME* journalist, sensing a real moral rapport, invited Charlie to condemn the recent soccer stud exposés in the Sunday tabloids as 'amazingly sexist', Charlie could be excused for permitting himself a wee blush.

Much of the resurgence of press interest in Charlie had to do with the relative improvement of form he had been enjoying all season. His deep-lying role between midfield and the strikers, was beginning to make sense and yield dividends.

Perhaps Don Howe wasn't quite the bungling Birmingham buffoon many took him for. Howe himself explained that the idea of such a role had first been brought into vogue by Hungary's Nador Hidegkuti. 'It's more difficult for opponents to pick him up and he has greater scope to run at the ball.'

Charlie had added his own spin having watched the great Michael Platini who had been pivotal in winning France the European Championships over the summer of 1984. 'It's all about vision. Look at the players who are the real crowd pleasers – these days – Hoddle, Souness, Dalglish – they are all players whose best talent is their vision,' he said.

Far from resenting the introduction of Paul Mariner, or

taking his signing as a slight against his own goalscoring abilities, Charlie welcomed the garrulous, cheery fellow, feeding off his jocular, fizzy presence in the dressing room. Charlie no longer felt stranded in the team – now he felt part of the team.

The upshot was a run of form with Mariner and Woodcock forming a working partnership upfront and Charlie filling in behind them, with Arsenal actually heading the table after a 4-1 win against Leicester. They slaughtered Liverpool with absurd finesse, Brian Talbot curling in a free kick as if he too had been watching Platini – though Platini himself would have done well to have watched and learned from this strike.

Come Christmas, with Arsenal still up there with a shout, Charlie crowned his year with a pair against Newcastle – the first a perfectly struck free kick, the second an almost comedic effort in which for once Lady Luck, one of the women with whom Charlie had had as much joy as he had Carolyn Seaward, finally smiled on him.

Woodcock drilled the ball across to Charlie whose shot deceived Carr in the Newcastle goal, only for the ball to hit the post and bounce back in off defender Roeder. Newcastle's defence was as impregnable then as it is today.

For Charlie, however, it seemed these good spells could never last for a fleeting few weeks or so. In January of 1985 Arsenal met York in the third round of the FA Cup. The giant killing of Arsenal was becoming an annual event by now, like a sort of seasonal morality play in which Arsenal were doomed to play Goliaths to an ever-plucky bunch of lower division Davids. The match was scrappily even until a late penalty, and, on a snowy pitch, with Keith Houchen to take the spot-kick, all that was missing was a drum-roll as York's doughtiest craned forward in the terrace behind John Lukic. He scored – and as York fans cheered like peasants at the guillotining of a French aristocrat, Don Howe was forced to sit in the dugout and endure a pelting of snowballs from disgruntled Arsenal fans.

It was Charlie who bore the backlash of this setback. Don Howe had already reprimanded him publicly after the 'birds'n' booze' débâcle, suspecting that Charlie's private life was out of hand. 'Sometimes I feel like I am whistling in the wind with him . . . he must remember that he carries the good name of Arsenal on his shoulders. He will always be in the public eye. He must mature and be more selective of his friends.' He'd already been dropped, for the first time in his career, as had Pat Jennings, for the first time in *his* career after a woefully inert performance against Sheffield Wednesday had been televised. And, though he'd bounced back against Newcastle, he'd not been able to pull his usual matchwinning stunt against Spurs at Highbury the following week and found himself beckoned into the dugout to make way for Steve Williams.

Charlie had been substituted again in the York débâcle and remained on the bench against Liverpool, where Arsenal went down 3-0, with Nicholas unable to pull back the requisite four after he was eventually brought on.

Don Howe deduced a link between Charlie's on-field performance and his 'Playboy image'. He was not the first manager to do so, though on closer inspection the charge seemed a little dubious. Fellow professionals always lauded Charlie as a good trainer. There had, of course, been those rumours in his previous tenure at Celtic that he'd missed a vital semi-final due not to the 'injury' that was the official explanation but to having been out on the piss and was therefore incapable. They remained just that, however, rumours. And there were no similar occurrences.

In spite of gossipy tales of laddish carousing, in spite of the alcoholic connotations of his wearisomely familiar nickname, Charlie Nicholas didn't have a reputation as a serious boozer. 'No one ever thought of him in that way when he was up here,' says journalist Phil Gordon. When Charlie called seven or eight pints 'not really being drunk', the more temperate element of the public might have boggled with incredulity but by footballing standards, he was probably about right. He was compared to George Best but Charlie knew where to draw the line. You'd never have seen him on TV, tiddly and giggly, clutching at Terry Wogan's knee to keep his balance like George. In any case, the game's real alcoholics weren't high-profile types who made whoopee around the ritziest nitespots playing cat and mouse with the paparazzi, but quiet, solid types who might never have been suspected of putting the stuff away by the pailful. Charlie was no Jim Baxter or Paul Merson.

Still, if he was far from a full-blown alcoholic, he was often far from his bed when he oughtn't have been. The next storm broke after Charlie had missed – by some considerable distance – an 11 pm curfew set by Jock Stein, a stern teetotaller, at the McDonald's hotel where Scotland were staying over in preparation for their next big fixture. Charlie and Glasgow chum Mo Johnston had decided that, tempting as the prospect of ping-pong and orange squash in the hotel lounge undoubtedly was, adventure might be sought further afield. They returned in the wee small hours after a fact-finding mission of the local hostelries had gone into extra time – and what happened after that is the subject of myth and speculation. One story has it that Charlie and Mo, stumbling in with much Ssshhing and fumbling for keys had run straight into big Jock sitting on a sofa in the lobby, glowering like Florrie in hair curlers clutching her rolling pin in the old Andy Capp cartoons. Another had it that, with the door to the hotel being locked, they'd rang at the buzzer, only for a little gent to appear and let them in. Whereupon Charlie had slipped a tenner into the fellow's breast pocket, as if to say, not a word to the big man, eh? The next morning, however, as the coach left for the plane with Charlie and Mo penitently nursing morning heads, they'd run into the little man who'd let them in the night before. He was an SFA official. And he didn't give Charlie his tenner back, either.

Jock Stein would neither confirm nor deny the stories. 'If you want to run a story, run it,' was his sole, gruff comment to the press pack. Not exactly a ringing endorsement of his young protégés. Charlie didn't make the cut for the next game against Iceland. 'In Iceland we will need men to work hard and get their heads down,' said Stein, inferring that men more interested in getting their beers down were of little use to him.

Somehow, things didn't seem to be going awfully well in the post-Bev Walker regime. Matters hadn't been helped by yet another motoring offence, speeding at 125 mph down the M62. Then in late February there had been reports that Charlie had demanded a £4000 fee to go out with 'punk heiress' Clara Willan – a straggle-haired peroxided art student whose aunt had bequeathed her a fortune – for which, said his agent, he promised a basic service of dinner and then on to a nightclub. 'It's quite pricey I admit,' his agent Frank Boyd had been reported as saying, 'but Charlie is in a high tax bracket.'

Later, Boyd insisted that the whole thing had been got up by the press, that he'd only been discussing a hypothetical figure to some tabloid hack and that Charlie had known nothing about the whole affair at all. But Boyd had been marked down as a disruptive influence and Charlie was informed that his agent was banned from Highbury, forthwith and indefinitely. In the eyes of some, if Charlie had hit rock bottom with Bev Walker, with Frank Boyd he had started drilling.

Charlie struggled to rediscover the wave of form on which he'd surfed through the first half of the season but he seemed to be increasingly out of sorts on the field of play. It had often been said that his appeal to fans was that they identified with him so strongly, saw him as one of their own out there. In a sense, that was true enough right now – he was basically a spectator on the pitch. Against Everton in March he could barely manage more than one shot on target, which Southall gathered into his arms like a friendly pup.

His slough of despond deepened when he was involved in an elbowing incident, which was blown up all over the back pages. To his string of iniquities – Champagne Charlie, Playboy Charlie, Proper Charlie – they now seemed bent on adding

Psycho Charlie. It was very infrequently that Charlie was involved in tear-ups, unlike cronies such as Mo Johnston. But the incident couldn't have come at a worse time.

If Charlie's image had taken a scuffing, the image of football was in the process of taking a near-mortal battering. 1985 was, indeed, football's annus horribilis. To start with, a series of disputes between the TV companies and the FA had put coverage of the game in jeopardy. With alternative sports such as snooker, athletics and boxing enjoying a rapid rise in the ratings, the TV companies had felt that football was pricing itself out of the market. There was the fire at Bradford's stadium, in which scores of fans had died in an inferno after a discarded cigarette ignited piles of papery rubbish beneath the terraces, with the wooden stand going up in flames within minutes. There had been an eruption of hooliganism, thought to have been dormant since the mid-seventies, culminating in a riot by Millwall fans at Luton's Kenilworth Road, prompting an instant, knee-jerk proposal of ID cards by Mrs Thatcher.

The events that transpired at the Heysel stadium in Brussels as Liverpool prepared to meet Juventus in the European Cup Final could never be forgotten though. BBC viewers were to see the game live after *Wogan* – and, in a naff link up, Terry and guest Bruce Forsyth were got up in Liverpool scarves and rosettes in the BBC studio, where they transferred from the interview set to a sofa in front of a TV set, like several million punters at home, to join Barry Davies live. The dubious levity of the scenario instantly evaporated as Davies was obliged to report that the game had been delayed due to the collapse of a wall. It slowly transpired that there had been fatalities – 38 in all – yet the game went ahead, to prevent further stampeding and confusion, with the players unaware of the full extent of the numbness and a growing sense of reproach at the obscenely trivial irrelevancy of football under these circumstances. Indeed, football had been to blame for the deaths, inculcating as it did a rampant, careless culture of boorish confrontation. Both left and right interpreted the events according to their own agendas. Some saw all of these tragedies as the upshot of neglect on the part of the football authorities and of the authorities at large – the first wages of the sins of the Tory ruling classes. Others, including of course Mrs Thatcher, saw it differently, with football fans as fair game to beat with the law-and-order stick.

Whatever, football, with a dwindling number of friends as it had, now had still fewer. One commentator – and he would have spoken for the reasonable many in 1985 – said that, if football were responsible for just one of these deaths, then the time had come to 'let football die'.

1985 wasn't a good year to be a footballer with a tarnished reputation. It was time for Charlie to get his act seriously together. It was time for new management and a clean-up.

Chapter Eight

Charlie had decided to put his affairs in the hands of Jerome Anderson, in conjunction with 'business adviser, nanny and minder' Mel Goldberg, and together they began a concerted charm offensive. He was featured visiting Great Ormond Street Hospital which was no wrench for him as his charity work had never let up behind the scenes. He was presented in the soft focus of the women's pages of the daily press, and a curiously post-modern exercise was undertaken in which Charlie gave interview after interview the main thrust of which was his explaining how he was in the process of polishing up his tarnished image for interviews. With an ironic grin, he explained that his favourite day of the week was now Sundays, as that was when he went to visit Graham Rix and his family for lunch.

'I'm envious of other people my age who are free to take girls out all the time and live it up,' he commented piously, to which every other lad his age must have snorted a collective 'Yeah, right!', 'but when I became a footballer I knew there were certain sacrifices I'd have to make.'

Over the next few months, he and his people put themselves to great pains to construct New Charlie. His recreations were listed as snooker with Paul Mariner, golf with his agent Jerome Anderson and the occasional quiet evening with Mike Peters of The Alarm, during which they discussed Arsenal FC and the state of Welsh indie-rock. Charlie's sister Janice came down from Scotland to share his flat – an important move, a strong connection with family that would stave off the deep-seated loneliness that had prompted him to seek warmth in the arms of a string of celebrity floozies, a rat-pack of dubious quaffing cronies and the odd blaze of paparazzi bulbs.

For the truth was that, in spite of a life apparently swaddled by glitz, champagne and adoring babes, Charlie was, for much of the time, pretty lonely in London. Danny Crainie, one of his old Celtic cronies, remembers, 'While I was at Wolves I'd often get calls from Charlie on a Saturday night complaining he was having to sit in with a bottle of wine and a video that night, because he'd no one to go out with. Most of the Arsenal boys had families.'

Indeed, so bereft of company was Charlie that it wasn't uncommon for him to drive up to Wolverhampton of a weekend, in spite of his early unpleasant encounter there, just for company with the old crowd. Same thing with Mike Conroy, who was up at Blackpool at this point: 'He'd drive all the way up to Blackpool, just to see a friendly face from the old days.'

Graham Rix, too, was often called upon to provide company

for Charlie. Like most garrulous people, Charlie loved any company other than just his own. Sometimes, all Charlie wanted was just a quiet pint at a local. Annabel's or Tramps, forget it. However, Charlie's and Graham's ideas of dressing for such an occasion weren't always congruent. 'I remember one time he was at a loose end and I'd agreed to meet him at my local,' says Graham. 'I rolled up in just my usual jeans, jacket and trainers – and Charlie arrives in a white leather suit. I said to him, 'Well, Charlie, one of us has got it wrong.'

There was a silly incident, early in 1986 when Charlie was accused of 'assaulting' a youngster during Arsenal's fifth-round draw against Luton. The lad's father even reported the matter to the police. But it was hardly Eric Cantona flying feet first Kung Fu-style into the crowd at Crystal Palace, more a case of pulling the boy's bobble hat over his ears, and the matter was dropped almost immediately. Ironically, after the same match, three fans were stabbed outside the ground and 32 arrests were made for violent disorder. But this was reduced to a footnote in most reports. The Charlie Nicholas non-incident was deemed to be of far greater significance.

Otherwise, on the field, Charlie had been having a pretty good time of things, although November had been a nightmare. He'd scored against Everton. But they'd hit six back, inspired by Lineker in a match at which no TV cameras whatsoever were present, such was the lukewarm relationship between TV and the game. Two 0-0 draws followed. The first, against West Bromwich Albion, ended up in a roasting by Don Howe for lack of effort. The second, against Birmingham, was declared by Nick Hornby to be 'surely the worst game of football ever played in the history of the First Division' – and somehow, you can imagine it might well have been. But Charlie often seemed to come to life around Christmas and raise his game against the big clubs. So it was this year. With a perversity typical of Arsenal during this entire era, they lost 3-0 to Southampton in early December – and then a week later turned over Liverpool at home. In this, Charlie Nicholas's 100th First Division game, he acquitted himself well. Graham Rix turned around a sluggish push forward by the Liverpool midfield and Charlie picked up the ball in the penalty box, where he skittered almost girlishly before slotting past Grobbelaar with ample space and time to spare.

A week later, it was Man Utd's turn up at Old Trafford which looked to be only a pint or so the right side of waterlogged. On the squelchy surface there was no shortage of slapstick. Norman Whiteside was trying to whack the ball clear from a sodden patch of turf, only for it to skid skew-whiff and bounce off the back of a team-mate's heels, breaking kindly for Quinn, who slid in against the keeper, only for the ball to bobble to Charlie. His arrogant little side-footer had just enough pace to clear the mud with the ball literally floating over the line for the only goal of the match. A further strike against QPR the following Saturday meant that Charlie went into Hogmanay as the club's top scorer thus far that season.

In January 1986 Charlie continued to hold his form. Two Brazilian-style freekicks from him were all that stood between Arsenal and yet another addition to their litany of embarrassing defeats to humble but dogged opposition as they eventually saw off Grimsby 4-3 in the FA Cup third round. And it was only Charlie's acumen in front of goal that kept Arsenal in the Milk Cup as both Graham Rix and Niall Quinn had such difficulty in shooting successfully from point blank range that the Villa keeper must have felt like Samuel L Jackson in *Pulp Fiction* – that the Lord had granted him a miracle.

This upsurge attracted the attention of Alex Ferguson, who had taken over as Scotland manager following the unhappy death of Jock Stein after the Scotland-Wales game months earlier. Jock Stein had never really known what to make of Charlie; the man had interests in a hairdressers, for Heaven's sake. This hadn't been the way they had done things at Dunfermline in the fifties. Given an hour alone with Charlie in a locked room, his impulse might well have been to ram his head down on a table, shave that stupid Bono hairstyle down to a two-bob-all-off crewcut, yank that stupid bit of metal out of his ear, then bark at him to get down on that stone floor and give him 200 squat thrusts.

Alex Ferguson was no student of the provocative effeminacies of eighties fashions himself and was rarely, if indeed ever, spotted up the front at Psychedelic Furs gigs. But he had a degree in player's psychology earnt at the University of Life, and knew, then as now, that different players needed different ways of geeing up, and felt that there was hope for Charlie Nicholas' career yet if he could get him in the right frame of mind to succeed. From the beginning of the year Ferguson was watching Charlie closely, with a view to figuring him in the plans for the 1986 World Cup in Mexico.

In the meantime, Charlie and Arsenal were about to enter what would eventually come to be seen as the end of an area of non-achievement. Don Howe had done a competent enough holding job at Arsenal in two and a half years, and while he never inspired much more than sporadic and half-hearted jeers of animosity from fans, nor did anyone ever imagine that Arsenal were ever going to be anything much more than the biggest small team in the First Division – or maybe the smallest big team. After 16 years, perhaps Howe was too close to the club to be able to conceive any grand vision for overhauling Arsenal's fortunes. The supporters, too, had almost come to accept Arsenal's status as fifth or sixth best as being as immutable a fact of life as the smallness of their pitch. Charlie had been drafted in to inject class and style, and while fans never wavered in their love for him, they could read the statistics as well as anyone. It had never quite happened.

The arrival on the board of millionaire David Dein and his money, however, had always augured the probability of big ideas and for weeks there had been strong rumours that Terry Venables, about to be freed from his ridiculously exacting employers at Barcelona, would be coming back to England, specifically to Arsenal, to bring his coaching nous and cock-sparrer swagger to bear on a club that, if not quite ailing, was certainly moribund.

Howe was aware of the rumours and he had his pride. He resigned, ironically, after a 3-0 defeat of Coventry that was Arsenal's fourth league win in a row, slighted but head held high. There being no further business to fight for in any of the competitions, the rest of the season tapered away in a sort of limbo.

For Charlie, however, potentially the biggest footballing challenge of his life was barely weeks away. For the fourth successive time, Scotland had qualified for the World Cup – and under their fourth successive manager. The story had always been the same. In 1974 they'd come within one goal and one minute of qualifying for the second phase. In 1978 Willie Johnston had tested positive for 'stimulants' after Scotland put themselves out against Peru – ironic, as he'd played throughout the game as if on a lethal cocktail of Night Nurse and Horlicks. In 1982, Scotland had shown one flash of brilliance when Narey snatched an astonishing opening goal from the edge of the box against Brazil before the latter, having matched Scotland's top gear, moved into their own second, third, then fourth.

Alex Ferguson was the new manager and was much more sympathetic to Charlie Nicholas than had been the late Jock Stein, who had hardly figured him in the qualifying matches, except for eight lively minutes against Spain. In a squad surprising for its absences – Chelsea's David Speedie, speedy of temper too, unfortunately; Kenny Dalglish, whose knees had gone; Mo Johnston (caught in a hotel room with two women); and, most curious of all, Alan Hansen. In fact, Charlie Nicholas was the only England-based player in the entire squad.

Scotland's first match was to be against Denmark, a country which now notable for four things – bacon, large dogs, beer and now out-and-out attacking football, under the aegis of former German international Sepp Piontek. With the likes of Jan Molby, Soren Lerby, Jesper Olsen and Michael Laudrup in their ranks, they were perhaps the most exciting side in Europe. Alex Ferguson hoped to shock-absorb their twin spearheads, with McLeish and Aitken marking Laudrup and Elkjaer. Meanwhile, upfront, he was looking to Strachan, Gough and especially Nicholas to play the Danes at their own game.

This was Charlie's first World Cup game in the starting line-up, and he intended to be worthy of it. Alex Ferguson had been boosting his self-belief and pumping up his adrenalin, 'I told him I want him to have the courage and the confidence to take on [the Danish] defenders because there is no doubt he can do so in any company.'

The match took place in Neza, an almost obscenely swish stadium, built as it was in the midst of some of Mexico City's most desperate, impoverished suburbs. Very little in the way of bright lights there. The first half was all Scotland, with Charlie on song and very nearly netting Scotland's openers as the Danes looked lethargic in the face of Scotland's energy and inventiveness. He was enjoying himself; the Danes weren't.

Come the second half, and Denmark reasserted themselves, with Laudrup and Elkjaer beginning to pick openings in the Scottish defence. They managed to rebuff the counter-attack but, with typical Scottish good fortune at this level, they conceded a goal after Elkjaer played a one-two off Willie Miller's legs and scored in off the post.

One or two heads dropped. Strachan went missing altogether and was eventually substituted, but Charlie's blood was up – his sixth sense for the occasion, the possible grandstand finalé sniffed glory and now the adrenalin was coursing through his veins as he continued to harry the Danish defence amidships. There were perhaps memories of Ajax for Jan Molby as the awkward Danes were time and again left trailing and flailing by Charlie's taunting runs – past one, over a second, round a third before crossing to Souness who, his instincts dulled a fraction with age, blasted it wide.

No matter. Back came Charlie again. The clock showed 82 minutes gone. The Danes were disconcerted and on the back foot as Charlie picked up the ball and invited his oppos to come and have a snatch if they thought they were fast enough. Klaus Berggren of Pisa loomed. Charlie nipped past him – but Berrgren lunged with cold pragmatism at his ankles, bringing him down in a pirouette of agony. Charlie let out a discordant scream. It was like bringing an anvil down on an exposed piano wire. His ankle ligaments were shattered, as were his dreams of turning the game and perhaps even the tournament for Scotland. Charlie afterwards described the grotesque foul, for which the Dane was not even booked, let alone sent off, as 'the worst tackle I have ever suffered in my life' – and that was saying something. As for Berrgren, his response afterwards was cold-eyed: 'I did what I had to do.'

Once more, Charlie had been 'done'. That he would take no part in the subsequent game against West Germany was self-evident. Scotland would lose that one, though Gordon Strachan had opened the scoring, and, more importantly, provided the image most would take home of Scotland's campaign that year as, in his excitement, he attempted to vault an advertising hoarding for which his legs proved too wee. The third game was a crunch one in every respect. Uruguay, a nation whose name never seemed to come up anywhere except in the context of football, fought, gouged, hacked and even pinched their way through to the 0-0 draw they needed. The first indication of the Corinthian spirit in which they intended to play the game came after 45 seconds when Quiniou was sent off for a Jackie Chan-style tackle on Gordon Strachan. Scotland were unable to make the most of the one-man advantage and were bundled unceremoniously out of the game. Charlie Nicholas, however, had astonishingly recovered sufficiently to make the substitute's bench, when the initial impact of the Danish tackle had made it seem likely that he would be reduced to crutches for the rest of his life. But the die was cast and he couldn't get into the game. Scotland were jeered off the pitch for not having made the best of their one-man advantage to cross the first hurdle – it was now four failures on the trot and fans, who were forced to cut short their holiday early once again, were getting exasperated. The Scottish management, however, were furious. One senior official talked about having had to play the 'scum of the world football', while Alex Ferguson publicly berated Uruguay manager Borras for a 'liar and a cheat' to his face at post-match press conference.

As with Celtic years earlier, Scotland could console themselves that they'd been moral victors, done down by the dirty dago. There'd be other tournaments. For Charlie Nicholas, however, this had been his best and perhaps his last chance, of which he'd been cheated out of by foul means.

Chapter Nine

As a player, George Graham had had a surprising amount in common with Charlie Nicholas. No one could have excused 'Stroller' of being a workhorse. His attitude towards the game was 'laid back, to say the least' by his own admission – he'd once nearly come to blows with an exasperated Frank McLintock in the tunnel, when the latter accused him of not pulling his weight. 'I'd never have picked myself for one of my teams!' he laughs today. But then, he raised his game well enough when it really counted – he'd been the decisive influence in the Arsenal-Liverpool Cup Final of 1971. The teams would meet, same place, in Charlie's final 16 years later.

Earlier, Graham had been at Chelsea, the team most associated with the King's Road-Swinging London scene of the late sixties and he had been one of the infamous Blackpool Eight, who, very Charlie-like, had broken an eleven o'clock hotel curfew during a week's training break and been roasted by manager Tommy Docherty. As with Charlie, he protests that tales of wild debauchery whipped up by the tabloids were exaggerated – in fact, the players had merely spent a late evening in a bowling alley with an after-hours bar. Indeed, had George worn a kaftan and dated Twiggy, he would have had the complete set of credentials for a Charlie prototype. But he didn't quite go that far.

On arriving at Arsenal, he'd developed a respect for the traditions of the club. 'I learned as a player that there was a Highbury way of doing things,' George Graham said in an interview at the time. 'All organisations must have a code of conduct, otherwise you get anarchy.' George very quickly became Arsenal Man.

On retiring as a player, he had a spell running the youth teams at Crystal Palace and QPR, and became a 'father figure' to the lads there – stern and encouraging by turns when necessary, hoping to instil in his young charges the importance of 'application and attitude'.

His first managerial job proper was at Millwall, where he rescued the team from relegation to Division Three and then moulded them into a team who would challenge for promotion, bringing along in his time such promising youngsters as Teddy Sheringham and John Fashanu. Millwall's reputation was principally for hooliganism, their resident band of thugs on the point of acquiring national notoriety with their pitch invasion at Luton. George Graham did all that he could to quell this element, meeting and berating them face to face on occasion. Ultimately, however, it was a social problem. What he could do was see that his players could not possibly be accused of setting a bad or slovenly example on the pitch and thereby inciting further degeneracy. To this end, he introduced a system of fines for any player pulled up for dissent or reckless play, unpunctuality and even going out on to the pitch without shinpads or with their shirts hanging out. Whether the sight of an upright Teddy Sheringham trotting out with his shirt tucked neatly inside his shorts did anything to pacify or morally improve Millwall's moronic element is hard to gauge – but a good deed in a naughty world never did any harm.

When George was allowed to leave Millwall to take up the Arsenal appointment in 1986, there was applause for a sensible choice but no great sense of an ecstatic new dawn. That Terry Venables had spurned the club was evidence to Arsenal of their essential plainness – and perhaps there was still a pro-Malcolm McDonald faction who hoped their chosen one might lead Arsenal out of the mid-table wilderness. Those with long memories or at least a rudimentary sense of their club's history would have venerated George Graham as a member of the double-winning side of 1971. But his profile had been so low over the past few years that there were one or two who wondered if maybe he'd been running a pub prior to the Millwall job. It had been hard to judge from his work there what sort of manager he would turn out to be although the initial impression was of a steady, prudent, unflamboyant stewardship, not the sort to lavish wads of Arsenal lucre on players in order to have the terraces doing the samba to a brace of these sensational flair players. Initially the most sensational it got was paying £50,000 for Perry Groves from Colchester.

What's more, Graham saw no reason to discontinue the

codes of conduct he'd established at Millwall. A TV interview he gave early on sounded almost like a recruitment for the military: 'Standards in British society are falling. I'm going to make sure they don't fall at Arsenal. I want ambitious young men with attitude, allied with skill.' His head-on experience with the thugs of Millwall, who were considered by many to be the early signs of a cancer that might wipe out the game, had left him with a horror of anything that might even be construed to smack of juvenile delinquency.

Into this category fell Charlie Nicholas's earring. That gold stud, which, to those not au fait with the mores of fashion seemed to betoken an arcane world of razzle-dazzle and debauchery, had to go, as part of Graham's campaign to smarten up the team. 'I've never liked players to look slovenly,' rapped the new manager. In his biography *The Glory And The Grief*, he describes calling Charlie into his office and instructing him to ditch the Champagne Charlie image: 'You're a super player but if you continue to live a faster life off the pitch than on it, I shall come down on you like a ton of bricks.' He also insisted on blazers and slacks on match days, before delivering a mini-*Face*-style editorial: 'The casual days are over.'

Charlie complied eagerly enough, perhaps embarrassed at this repeat of the treatment he'd received at the hands of Billy McNeill when barely out of his teens. Fine. No point in making a fuss about an earring . . .

Charlie was at pains to impress his new manager who clearly regarded him with slightly narrowed eyes. It didn't help, therefore, when tabloid surveillance cameras caught him cavorting with a 'bubbly blonde beauty' at 3.30 am on what he insisted was an increasingly rare visit to Stringfellows. It being August, the tabloids were ravenous for such morsels, however, and Charlie was caught, so to speak, with his hand in the cookie jar, glowering daggers – for Heaven's sake, what was wrong with enjoying yourself? Pretty innocuous stuff, all this and hardly the sort of decadence that was liable to put civilisation in jeopardy – but George Graham responded with a ban on his players from West End nightclubs and from drinking two nights before matches. 'London's a big place,' says George today. 'It's easy for players to hide and not easy to keep track of them.'

Much more serious and damaging to Charlie was a court case which dredged up an incident which had supposedly taken place two years earlier, while Charlie had holidayed with friends in Ibiza's San Antonio. Student Lori McElroy, then 26, from West Glasgow, brought a civil action against Charlie at Westminster County Court. She alleged that Charlie, accompanied by Willie McStay and three other friends had approached Ms McElroy and her boyfriend Brendan Murphy as they were eating from a bag of chips outside the Confusion Bar. He'd nicked a chip from their bag and Ms McElroy, recognising him, had retorted, 'Listen, Charlie, we're not impressed. Go and pester someone else.' Whereupon, she testified, Charlie flew into a rage, punching her on the jaw. As she turned round, she was aware of Charlie being restrained by his mates, 'his legs flailing out towards me'. As well as restraining Charlie, however, she alleged that Charlie and cronies beat up her boyfriend who sustained a broken rib – the evidence of this was presented in professional-looking agency photos which the papers had received in summer of 1984, featuring both Ms McElroy and her bandaged boyfriend.

Charlie protested that while a chip had certainly been purloined by one of his party, he and Willie McStay had had nothing to do with the subsequent mêlée – as professional footballers used to being recognised in the street, they knew the best way to deal with these sorts of 'hassles' was simply to walk away from them. Charlie's defence team, however, did present a witness, Christopher Brown, 24, unemployed, of Brixton, who insisted that it was he who had slapped Ms McElroy and pushed her away to defend Charlie. He denied that he was simply being 'set up to take the rap for the footballer'.

Judge Denis McDonnell was singularly unimpressed by Mr Brown. His evidence, he surmised, was 'a pack of transparent lies'. He was still less impressed by Charlie. He described the assault on Ms McElroy as an 'arrogant, nasty and cowardly assault' of which Charlie was certainly guilty: 'I am old fashioned enough to think that it is particularly nasty for a man to strike a woman – especially an athletic man.' He suggested meaningfully that 'it may well be that Mr Nicholas had not been fully in control of himself'.

Charlie insisted that he had only had two pints of lager on the night in question but to no avail. He was ordered to pay Ms McElroy £1,300 in damages.

Charlie's team immediately launched an appeal which they subsequently dropped, so the judge's verdict remains the last official word on this matter.

Certainly, however, those who knew Charlie were surprised

and puzzled by the incident. Given that Charlie's profile was a high one and he was spotted out at pubs and clubs so often, this was the first time a fracas like this had risen to the surface. It didn't seem in his nature. In spite of frequent provocations his disciplinary record on the pitch was respectable enough and in spite of his cocky and conspicuous persona he had always evaded any serious bother with idiots in pubs. Mo Johnston had a record of being involved in violent altercations that was as long as your arm, as would Gazza later on, and it was easy enough to draw your own conclusions from that. These sorts of incidents usually came in sixes, sevens, eights, but a one-off? Nothing of the sort ever appeared on Charlie's record again.

The stain on Charlie's character wouldn't be lightly over-looked by George Graham, however, and now he had it all to do on the pitch. Upfront partners such as Woodcock and Mariner had already been let go, the former to depart for Cologne, the latter on a free transfer. Younger players had their contracts renewed but the message to everyone was, get with the pro-gramme. 'The Arsenal shirt must be worn with pride,' said Graham. 'You have to earn the right to wear it.' Especially on the sort of wages this Arsenal team were commanding, in some cases ten times what Graham had taken home himself as a player at Arsenal. No names mentioned, but Graham would have no truck with 'prima donnas'. The emphasis, at all times, was on the team.

Charlie made a good start however. The first game of the new season was at home against Man Utd, and Arsenal sneaked it late on 1-0, with Charlie making a relatively uncommon incursion into the six-yard box and grabbing a tap-in. It was just the spirit Graham was looking for – getting in there, terrier-after-a-rat-type stuff, rather than loitering on the edge of the box, aloof from the fray. However, defeats against Coventry and Liverpool followed and the Clock End began to hum with low murmurs of frustration. Three 0-0 draws followed, against Spurs, Luton and Oxford Utd and chants of 'interesting, interesting Arsenal!' reached an all-time low. No one could work out why Graham wasn't putting his hands into the pockets of those grey slacks and shelling out. It seemed hard to see how he could build a winning team with mere injunctions to the existing players to keep a straight back and their shirts tucked in.

Worse followed, especially so for Charlie, in the following 1-0 defeat against Nottingham Forest, as Charlie, orders from his manager to get more involved in the opposition penalty box doubtless ringing in his ears, went flailing in for a 50-50 collision with Forest keeper Steve Sutton. Charlie came off worst as a searing gash tore up through his right leg and he crumpled into an anguished heap.

'I knew that it was a bad injury,' said Charlie. 'I looked down and could actually see right inside my leg. The cut went through several layers of skin. A fraction to one side and it could have ripped all my ligaments.'

Initially, Charlie had feared that the gash might be career-threatening. As it was, he would be out for the next seven weeks, with only grapes and good wishes to console him.

How heartily Charlie cheered as Arsenal, in his absence, went on to show a thunderous flash of form is uncertain. 3-1 against Watford. 2-1 against Newcastle United. 3-1 against Chelsea. 2-0 against Charlton. 4-0 against Southampton. 3-0 against Manchester City. 4-0 against Southampton. It was the younger bucks – Hayes, Adams, Rocastle, Quinn and Groves who were making all the running, developing the beginnings of a coherence and understanding that promised to lead to big things. Charlie looked on with a mixture of feelings, indispensability not included among them.

Both Charlie and Graham Rix, who had recovered from an Achilles tendon operation, now found they couldn't get back in the team. 'If I put them straight back in the side I would lose all credibility in what I am trying to achieve,' said George Graham. Arsenal were at this point on a run of 13 games without defeat. It would extend to 17 and come the turn of the year, they would head the table.

For Charlie, the sole consolation of this period was the year-early rescinding of his driving ban. His lawyers went to Glasgow court and argued that, since he had no car, Charlie had been encumbered in carrying out his charity work. From most footballers, this would have sounded like the most pricelessly pious guff in legal history and been guffawed out of any competent court. But there was no doubt that Charlie had always enthusiastically taken on more than his fair share of hospital visits and the like, and Sheriff James Jardine was sufficiently impressed with Charlie's 'new mature outlook'. He could drive again.

The court may not have been so impressed that Charlie, in anticipation of a positive decision, had two weeks earlier ordered an £11,000 custom-built Porsche, which he was able to collect practically the moment the verdict went his way. Still the cheeky chappie.

He was beginning to develop a streak of outspokenness. As well as testing his bargaining strength by hinting that he might fancy joining Ian Rush, whose transfer to Juventus at the end of the season had been announced, in Italy, Charlie commented pointedly on the contrastingly moribund state of the British game. 'I'm not the type to hold anything against George Graham but I've obviously got my opinion and I feel I should voice it. I just feel that the skilful player is losing out to the serial and workmanlike player,' he complained.

Charlie was a rare commodity, Charlie argued. But would George Graham appreciate how much he needed him?

What had peeved Charlie was Graham's high-ball tactics – they had achieved a run of success by the expedient of hoofing the ball upfield in the expectation that Niall Quinn, who at 6'4" was among the first footballers to know when it was raining, would be the first to get on the end of it. Charlie wasn't an aerial player, and never really had been. Perhaps he feared that excessive heading of the ball was bad for his precious follicles. Whatever, his magic was in his feet, 'The close controls, the double shuffle, the short back swing on the shot' as sportswriter Ian Archer once put it. Graham had often decried the churlishly physical, blunt, direct nature of the English game, especially with cloggers like Watford up there in the First Division. However, until Heysel had resulted in a ban on English clubs playing in Europe, the likes of Forest, Villa and especially

Liverpool had enjoyed an almost unbroken run of success in the European Cup alone, engendering an age-old confidence that plain, direct John Bull was worth a half dozen mincing foreign types and their fancy footwork. He wanted the ball to feet and, preferably, without snow on it. Charlie felt frozen out of Arsenal. 'We don't want a reputation as an attractive team that doesn't win matches,' said one Arsenal player at the end of the year – as if there were any danger. Moreover, Charlie felt frozen out of the English game. No wonder he dreamt wistfully of warm Italian climes.

But then, Arsenal's season took as equally dramatic a turn for the worse as it had earlier done for the better, when they lost 2-0 in a fractious game with Man Utd, when Rocastle was sent off and George Graham very nearly forgot his own codes of conduct and almost popped one on Alex Ferguson in the tunnel afterwards. There followed then a run of eight games without victory as Arsenal were found out. Niall Quinn was left on his own upfront as George Graham, even with £700,000 from the sale of Stewart Robson, tut-tutted at the scandalously inflated price of modern players and cannily bided his time.

Still there was no place for Charlie, forced to knock hatfuls in in reserve games. 'He's just lost a bit of his sparkle,' commented Graham, and tabloid headliners lunged gleefully into their grab-bag of 'CHAMPAGNE CHARLIE LOSES FIZZ'-type headlines. They sensed a conflict in the offing between Charlie and Graham and fanned it along nicely with a series of disproportionately copious features.

Still, Nicholas lifted his cup game, scoring one of the six

against Plymouth Argyle, another team who would pay dearly for Arsenal's humiliations at the hands of the minnows. His goal was reminiscent of one of George Best's classics against Spurs, with Charlie driven wider and wider by the defence before swivelling abruptly and slamming in a right-footer from a narrow angle. Charlie went on to score a typically well-coiffeured goal against Barnsley in the next round, but he'd come on as a sub, his backside burning scorchmarks of simmering indignation on the bench. By now, Charlie didn't know what to do. His love affair with the fans was mutually unabated and he didn't want to cause ructions, but another part of him was gasping for recognition and rehabilitation. Speculation ripened that come the end of the season, Charlie would be on his way.

Arsenal had also made good progress in the Littlewoods Cup, though Charlie had had a quiet tournament. The two-leg semi-final, however, against Spurs, looked to be the sort of fixtures that would sit up for him nicely. The home tie at Highbury was a disappointment, with Spurs taking the game to Arsenal with a curling Glenn Hoddle free-kick, Chris Waddle running rings around Gus Caesar and Nicholas standing up the other end wondering when Arsenal were going to carry the game to him.

Eventually, a Clive Allen goal put Spurs one-up and the Cockerels were pretty damn cocky in the return game at White Hart Lane as Clive Allen scored another one, making the aggregate 2-0. With Spurs practically doing victory rolls as their attacking formations continued to surge forward, their tannoy announcer engaged in what has now become a legendary bout of hubris, smirkingly giving out details of where Tottenham fans could acquire tickets for the final.

The wrath this incurred in the Arsenal team matched that of Henry V when France's Constable dispatched a consignment of tennis balls to his court. In other words, we weren't having any of that. The Gunners roared back, Charlie roaring as hard as anybody, pikestaffs aloft, and scattered the now flustered Spurs defence, and Viv Anderson and Niall Quinn pulled back to push the score into extra time and eventually force a replay, again at White Hart Lane, as George – by now, he was very definitely George, our George – lost the toss. The replay was a replay in every respect, with the same scoreline. Allen scored yet again for Spurs, and Arsenal, who must have felt like Bill Murray in *Groundhog Day*, had it all to do again. But Nicholas played no further part after a knock saw him stretchered off. There wasn't exactly a surge of expectation as moustached journeyman Ian Allinson trotted on in his place. Yet Allinson it was who scuffed in a shot whose slowness deceived everyone including Allinson himself – and, most importantly, Ray Clemence, as the ball put-putted home. 1-1! And then, in the absolute dying seconds, Rocky Rocastle took his place in folklore as he chested down the ball and volleyed home a winner that lit up the skies of north London with Arsenal ecstasy.

Arsenal were through to the Littlewoods Cup Final. But as news broke that George Graham had finally made his move in the transfer market and picked up Leicester City striker Alan Smith for £750,000, the future didn't look so red, white and rosy for Charlie.

Chapter Ten

The Littlewoods Cup semi-final triumph over Spurs had been a three-course banquet of joy for beleaguered gooners. Victory in the final over Liverpool was sweet indeed. Arsenal, unloved, derided and under-regarded, had shoved it back to their grinning, hateful detractors with interest. No one outside Highbury wanted to see the preening, elegant cockerels of Spurs overturned by Arsenal but with the odds against them and no one but each other to look to for encouragement, they'd done it just the same. It had been assumed that in the final, Arsenal would simply do the respectful thing and lay down and die in front of Liverpool, cultured ambassadors for English football. Not only had they beaten them but they'd done so even after Ian Rush had scored. Such insolence was an offence to the gods, a disobedience of natural law. Irritatingly, people were going to have to think again about Arsenal, especially under their new manager, this Graham fellow.

For Arsenal fans, it was like someone had reconnected the

power. The generators were humming once more, the lights were back on again. The victory had been doubly great insofar as Charlie Nicholas had scored the goals. Shin'ins, admittedly and it was debatable as to whether the second one wasn't perhaps an own goal. But there was something charming and cheeky about the sheer dodginess of the efforts. That was all it had taken to unseat yer high and mighty Liverpool. Just wait till we really got going.

Perhaps this would be the beginning of a new era. Perhaps this long-awaited triumph was a harbinger not just for an upturn in Arsenal's fortunes but an upturn in Charlie Nicholas's. After all, he was only 25 and with a bit of silverware under his belt, and maybe finally he would begin to fulfil his potential at Highbury.

You just never knew. That was one of the things that fans always so loved about Charlie. You just never knew what he was going to do next. And Charlie knew that, thick and thin, on good days and bad, the fans were always on his side. Even back in December, coming off the subs bench for ten minutes against QPR in his first appearance for several weeks due to injury, several weeks in which a Charlie-less Arsenal had turned round their form and won virtually every game handsomely, he was given a rapturous reception by fans, as if to say, 'Thank God you're back!'

As he began negotiations with George Graham regarding his future at Highbury, Charlie knew that goodwill, as well as that pair of goals in the Littlewoods Cup Final, would be among his key bargaining chips. It wasn't more money he was looking for as such – rather, a degree of security. He went public with a whole series of newspaper interviews, the common refrain of which was how much he loved Arsenal, how much he liked to think that the feeling was mutual, but, y'know, it was just a matter of arriving at sensible terms. While never less than enthusiastic about George Graham, and the exciting future he seemed to promise for Arsenal, Charlie suggested that he was a player of special needs, which previous regimes had neglected. 'Players like me, who are skilful and unpredictable, need encouragement. We need to be told, this is your role, play to your strengths.' Only then, he said, would the 'real' Charlie Nicholas emerge rather than the Charlie they'd seen wandering lonely and desolate like a lost soul in purdah upfield, giving futile pursuit to 60-yard high balls. And if Arsenal didn't want Charlie, well, there were plenty of clubs who did. Liverpool, as always, were a name in the frame, though he might not now be too popular in that part of the world for obvious reasons – and there would doubtless be forever a berth with his name on it in brass if he should ever decide to return to Celtic. They were likely to be recruiting for strikers, with Mo Johnston baulking on renewing his contract for the club.

George Graham was magnanimous enough towards Charlie and it had certainly not hurt him to commend Charlie on his 'magnificent' performance against Liverpool. But it had been, he stressed, a great team performance. George was only interested in the team. A team he was considering bolstering with possible future signings of the likes of John Sheridan and Brian Marwood. He'd also made enquiries about Watford's John Barnes and Kerry Dixon.

All the same, it did look as though Charlie and Arsenal would be able to agree terms that would keep him at the club into the nineties. By June, he was on the point of signing a new four-year contract. There was, however, a stumbling block – the signing on fee. George Graham, himself on a basic salary that fell some £20,000 short of Charlie's, had his own ideas about what constituted a sensible sum and it fell more than a bob or two short of what Charlie and agent Jerome Anderson considered the two-goal Cup Final hero, darling of the North Bank, was worth. As George Graham went off on his holidays, the situation was in stalemate with Charlie left to stew – and flutter his eyelashes hinting at other prospective suitors. A 'top Italian club' were said to be in the running to gather him up and sweep him off abroad if negotiations did fall through. And, with Mo Johnston en route for Nantes and Brian McClair off to Man Utd, Celtic were said to be prepared to pay Charlie the sort of signing on fee commensurate with his star status. Billy McNeill was back in the saddle up there – 'Charlie's the best player I ever worked with,' he effused.

George Graham didn't budge. But Christ, Celtic were offering him more money! Still, no word from George. In July, Charlie, realising that Mohammed was going to have to go to the mountain, had a last-ditch meeting with the Arsenal manager.

Graham himself wasn't having the best of luck with his own shopping quests. Watford had given him the polite raspberry as regards John Barnes. He'd been taken by QPR's Terry Fenwick, but on inspection of the £500,000 price tag George had drawn away with a sharp intake of breath. He'd made overtures to Brian

Marwood but the Sheffield Wednesday management had placed themselves bodily between George and the latter, declaring, 'Hands off!'

Charlie and George thrashed out a compromise which seemed to favour the manager rather than the player – a 12-month contract on unchanged terms. Charlie now talked up the challenge he now faced of fighting for and winning his place in the team, to prove the doubters wrong.

Said George Graham, 'He's a quality player. You can't have too many of them.' A glowing tribute but subtly inferring that Charlie was a luxury rather than an essential component of New Arsenal.

The 1987-88 season saw the arrival, at last, of Alan Smith. Far from him replacing Charlie, the idea was that they would form a partnership upfront. Both were in the starting line-up. But the fixture list saw Arsenal thrown, not mixing metaphors unjustifiably, into boiling waters at the deep end among the sharks. Liverpool and Man Utd would be their first two opponents. It was tough luck on Charlie. Liverpool came down to Highbury and, in front of 55,000 hopeful fans gave the Gunners a cursory 2-1 hiding, revenge for April and Wembley. Arsenal managed to repel boarders up at Old Trafford with a 0-0 draw but Charlie had been replaced with Perry Groves. Nick Hornby was among those Arsenal fans who suspected Charlie's bag of magic tricks would never quite suffice at this level any more. Fundamentally, he lacked pace. 'There were a few people saying that he just wasn't quick enough. We realised he wasn't going to pull off solo miracles.'

Chapter Ten

Charlie would have another chance in the starting line-up against QPR. It would, however, prove to be his last. Remembers Nick Hornby, 'We lost the match 2-0 – but Charlie did get a chance, in the box, which he fluffed. The thing is, it wasn't just that he fluffed it – there was a feeling among fans that he could have scored if he'd been willing to pitch in there, boots flying.'

Maybe Charlie's heart wasn't in the team any more. What was for certain is that Charlie himself wasn't in the team any more. He had died, sadly and alone, in a foreign field – well, Loftus Road, anyway. 'He was dropped for the next game against Portsmouth,' recalls Alan Smith laconically, 'and, er, unfortunately, we won it 6-0. Charlie'd probably have got a few goals as well but it wasn't to be.' He modestly omits to mention his own contribution of a hat-trick.

It was unfortunate indeed that with Charlie reduced to the reserves, Arsenal would once again embark on a dazzling run of form. After a 1-1 draw against Luton, Arsenal beat Nottingham Forest, Chelsea and Norwich. Goals scored in those games, 22; goals conceded, five. In the face of such impressive statistics, it wasn't easy for Charlie to argue for a recall on his mandate as people's champion. 'By now,' says Nick Hornby, 'the trust and sympathy had moved to George Graham. The club was back on course.'

Charlie couldn't command a place in the first team but he could still command an impressive stack of column inches in the tabloids. Realising that the point of no return had been reached, Charlie's 'stunning' transfer request was slapped on George Graham's desk with a blazing fanfare from the dailies. And, for the first time, Charlie admitted a point others had long since laboured into the ground: 'I made a mistake coming to Arsenal.'

Fearful of a protracted state of limbo, Charlie made a series of vigorous, cooing overtures to Liverpool and Celtic. 'When Liverpool come for you they usually get their man. I must have been one of the few who said no – and I must have been mad.' But Liverpool, with Beardsley, Aldrige and Barnes were plentifully stocked upfront, thank you, as they would prove later that season when they cut Nottingham Forest to pieces 5-0 in probably the greatest ever performance by an English club team. Celtic and Billy McNeill, meanwhile, had cooled somewhat, miffed that Charlie had spurned their generous advance the previous summer. Blow him. 'It's none of my business at the moment what is going on between Charlie and his club,' sniffed McNeill, jilted once and now not anxious to chase after a lukewarm property. As if purely out of scornful sarcasm, McNeill instead acquired another Charlie – Inverness's Charlie Christie, for £20,000.

There was, however, apparently one interested party. Scottish players were quite the rage in France that season, with Mo Johnston and Mark Hateley both having settled at Nantes and Monaco respectively. Racing Club of Paris, anxious to be at the leading edge of chic, made enquiries about Charlie Nicholas. The problem was that it seemed George Graham was determined to ensure that Arsenal got back as much of the £650,000 that had been paid for him as they could. Racing Club melted away from the reckoning – but then in stepped Toulon from the French Riviera.

This was a tempting one for Charlie. Toulon were a struggling team but they had a healthy war chest and fanatical support. Plus, they were situated on the French Riviera, a mere speed-boat's distance from Hately and golfing buddy Glenn Hoddle at Monaco. You'd have to fancy it, wouldn't you?

Interest went so far as talks between Arsenal's managing director Ken Friar and his opposite numbers at Toulon on October 12, and Jeff Powell in the *Daily Mail* felt sufficiently con-fident to report that a deal, negotiated in US dollars, would be confirmed the next day, worth a million bucks each to Charlie and Arsenal. At that day's Thomas Cook rates, that would mean Arsenal were only losing out £100,000 or so on what they'd paid for him.

Some busybody at the French end must have acquired a bundle of old tabloid cuttings, however, because only a day or so later, after a special board meeting, Toulon had a rather abrupt change of heart. They demanded a cut in the transfer fee and for Charlie to play out an eight-month probationary period. If he didn't hack it, he'd be on the next ferry back to England, with Toulon guaranteed their money back. They were worried, it was said, about Charlie's 'fun-loving' image. The last thing the Riviera needed, they reckoned, was another playboy.

Needless to say, Arsenal refused this revised deal – who did Toulon think they were, Victor Kayam? Money back guarantee, my left foot! So that was that, with Charlie and Jerome ruing once again the mythical aroma of sleaze and whoopee that still malingered about 'Champagne Charlie'.

George Graham offered Charlie an olive branch of sorts. If he played well enough for Arsenal reserves he might yet win back his place in the first team. The offer seemed almost like a taunt. Charlie didn't withdraw his transfer request. But interest was evaporating by the day. Celtic, having just splashed out £800,000 on Frank MacAvennie were clearly out of the 'race', though some race it was, with all participants speeding away in reverse gear. Feeling desperate and perhaps a little humiliated, Charlie protested that he was being priced out of the market – possibly deliberately, he hinted, as part of a mysterious vendetta on the part of George Graham. 'The manager never speaks to me except to offer the occasional 'Hello'. I'm not allowed to train with the first team. It's very tough . . . I don't know why George has done this to me.' Charlie had scored seven goals in six games for the reserves but, he grumbled, he would never make it back into the first team. 'George will never pick me.'

He was so desperate, Charlie said, that he was even considering an offer from Derby. 'To be honest, I will go anywhere to be part of first team football again.' He was suffering agonies sitting out the 12-month contract he'd ill-advisedly signed with Arsenal the previous summer and longed to be a free agent once more.

There was the prospect of Charlie going on loan to Derby – but Arsenal turned them down. It was hard not to suspect that George was deliberately teaching Charlie Nicholas a lesson in humility. This was exacerbated when he hit back at Charlie at the Guinness Sports Writers' Lunch in December. 'Look at Charlie's scoring record in Scotland and compare it with his record in England . . . what people tend to forget is the fact that we won ten consecutive games without him. Name me a manager who would change his team for any player in those circumstances, no matter what his skill.'

As for the idea that Charlie had won the Liverpool Cup for Arsenal, George said, 'Yes, he scored two goals but ten other players did quite well that day too.'

As for Charlie's much vaunted star status, snorted Graham, 'If you are a star then you have to perform.' And he compared him with the emergent Martin Hayes, another player, whom, George reminded his audience, had been dropped when he hit poor form – and no one had made a fuss about that. 'As far as I'm concerned, Charlie is no bigger a star than Martin Hayes.'

Ooooh!! Many of the writers begged to differ with that last crack – after Champagne Charlie, what price Martini Martin in the cocktail cabinet of footballing characters? But even those closest to Charlie's cause found it hard to argue that Arsenal were struggling without him.

After yards and yards of tabloid speculation, return flights to the Riviera, much bandying of big-name clubs such as Liverpool, Celtic, Racing Club of Paris and mysterious Italian teams, after all the hype and babble and mooted six-figure fees, Charlie sat out his 26th birthday facing the prospect of going back to Scotland – not even to his beloved Celtic but to Aberdeen, for a modest £400,000, which Arsenal had accepted.

Ex-footballers writing weekly columns lined up to form a hollow arch of hatchets as Charlie prepared to make his exit from English football. Said Emlyn Hughes, 'If Charlie is truthful with himself, he can look back on his Highbury career and think he could have done better.

'When I saw him recently he was still a little overweight, with a backside that needed trimming down. Perhaps he needs a return to Scotland – because it's easier to score goals north of the border – and I'm being cruel to be kind when I say that's where he should be.

'So go now, Chas, before it's too late.'

Wrote Johnny Giles in the *Daily Express*, 'Charlie Nicholas has become a tragic figure. Arsenal fans convinced themselves that he was a star. But Charlie isn't a star, never has been and – in the English First Division – never will be.

'If he isn't doing something spectacular, he isn't doing anything at all . . . the really influential players, the men who can dictate the game, get by with two touches. Charlie needs three. It is that need for a little extra time that sees him dispossessed more often than he should be.

'I just don't believe he has the all-round ability to be a dominant player in the First Division.'

Even one or two fans remarked that Charlie was surplus to requirement and even that they had been let down. 'The one thing supporters don't like is stars who earn £2000 a week, then bleat. For that money they should be sweating blood for the people who sweat blood to afford the seats.'

Says Nick Hornby, 'I always used to hate it when the press said that Charlie had come to the wrong club in Arsenal. After all, he did play under three different managers and he didn't fit in with any of them. And the truth is, he did go missing in matches.'

George Graham today plays down the notion that he and Charlie simply didn't get on. 'A lot of what you read in the press at that time about me and Charlie not getting on was just the media. Tabloids love to make things personal. I never had any problems with Charlie. All I wanted was a successful team – preferably with Charlie in it. And Charlie was in and out of the team even before I got to Arsenal. He'd never known what his best position was, whether to play upfront or behind the front two. And that was the case before I got there. But he was very popular with the fans and I always recognised that. I didn't fall out with Charlie, I've met him since he moved away from the team and we got along fine. But for all of that talk of interested clubs and Italy and France, at the end of the day only one firm offer came in and that was from Aberdeen.'

So that was that. Aberdeen. Charlie might have been expected to have felt relief at his early reprieve from a 12-month contractual limbo. He didn't. He later described the day he left Arsenal as 'the worst day of my career'.

In 151 appearances for Arsenal he scored only 34 goals. But he had always loved the fans, who had never got on his back. As for the players, in spite of very early rumours about resentful colleagues refusing to pass the ball to him, the truth was he was a real Arsenal player's player who inspired enormous affection in everyone who played alongside him. A garrulous, livewire, all'singing, all jesting prankster, he was always an immensely popular dressing'room presence, breaking pre-match tension with his raucous comic relief and galvanizing energy buzz, fending off a barrage of dodgy cracks about 'Jock The Lad', mercilessly hilarious derision of his latest leather designer outfit and leery queries about which page three bird he'd been sleeping with this week, and coming back with as good as he got. There was no animosity about him – in spite of reports that Alan Smith had been brought in to replace him, Smith today remembers him with nothing but affection, a 'real character and practical joker. He never shut up.'

Remembers Graham Rix, one player with whom Charlie forged a particularly close friendship – he's godfather to Graham's daughter – 'Charlie was loved, anyone will tell you that. And the players always got really, really protective of him when we went away from home and he got a barracking from away fans.'

As Charlie picked up the last of his things at Highbury, however, and made the short drive away from the ground for the last time, he couldn't help but feel high, dry, unwanted and very, very lonely. He was leaving behind thousands of friends, either personal or in spirit, knowing that he had never really given them everything they had so fervently hoped of him.

Says Tom Watt, 'It was funny. There was a great feeling for Charlie among the fans but at the same time no one was saying, oh no, we can't let him go. We loved him and yet we weren't sorry to see him go, if that makes sense.'

Charlie had made mistakes, overplayed his charisma card, but in spite of a few pesky paparazzi, he'd enjoyed the limelight, the constant affection and attention. He had his detractors too, of course, who had every reason to feel vindicated – and, ringing in his ears as he made that last car journey, were their declarations that at 26, Charlie was washed up as a top-flight footballer. No bevy of beauties or Roy of the Rovers cardboard cut-outs were there to wave him good-bye.

He couldn't help it. 'As I drove along I was almost blinded by tears,' he confessed later. 'It was just a half-hour journey but it felt like a day.'

By teatime, Charlie Nicholas was in Aberdeen.

Chapter Eleven

If this were fiction, we'd see Charlie Nicholas now, alone on an indifferently grey and rainswept day, a single knapsack flung dejectedly over the back of a faded leather jacket, standing alone on the first junction of the M1, holding up a soggy piece of cardboard with 'SCOTLAND' scrawled on it, a single, haunting bagpipe skirling out an elegiac note in the background.

In truth, of course, that lachrymose half-hour car journey was a brief hiatus before he was cast once again into a busy schedule of press conferences, interviews and public appearances as he set about rebuilding his career up at Aberdeen. Then manager Ian Porterfield was jubilant at his £400,000 coup. 'Charlie's the kind of player who turns draws into victories,' he said. 'He will add colour to our side and I believe in him totally.' Added vice-chairman Ian Donald with a dreamy glint in his eye, 'We haven't had a colourful character at Pittodrie since Gordon Strachan.' Those had been bleak years indeed. And right now, Aberdeen needed a splash of something upfront. Although they had the third-best defensive record of any British team, in 1987-88 they were the lowest scoring team in the Scottish Premiership. And they'd just lost striker Davie Dodds to injury.

Interest in Charlie had never abated in Scotland and the press conference room at Pittordrie was groaning with jostling journalists and clicking cameramen. Questions regarding reports that Charlie's career had suffered because of his off-the-field reputation were dissuaded by agent Jerome Anderson. The past was the past. Said Charlie, 'I'm old enough and wise enough not to worry about what the papers say.'

And so, Charlie wouldn't have been worried when, at the end of January 1988, his erotic and erratic past came back to bite him one last time. 'Stunning', 'pint-sized beauty' Theresa Bazar had had a couple of hits with breathy, peroxide, chromium-thin pop duo Dollar back in the early eighties. Unsurprisingly, the combo fairly quickly ran out of musical ideas and were discarded by the record buying public like a pair of paper lace underwear. Ms Bazar, however, hadn't run out of patience with the attentions of the newspapers and was a regular and co-operative presence in the tabloid pages for many years, well into the late eighties when Dollar records could only be obtained for 35p in newsagents' singles racks. The more spurious the story, the more prominent was the accompanying photo of Ms Bazar, all lipstick and bustiers. In 1988, the *News of the World* ran a series of her exposes on her nights out – and in – with her numerous and notable gentleman friends. She ranked them in order of impressiveness. And, while the likes of Duran Duran's John Taylor and Herr Flick from TV's '*Allo, 'Allo* merely received honourable mentions for the merits of their unmentionables, top of the Tree of Tumescence sat a proud Charlie Nicholas. Accompanied by a photo of Charlie taken from the 'Birds, Booze and Me' session in the same paper years earlier, bare chested, an inch of paunch peeping over his white trousers, the text saw Theresa gush appreciatively about Charlie's attentiveness as a lover.

With Theresa a guest at Highbury's director's box, there to study recent form, she'd found herself chatted up by Charlie at the post-match reception. They then headed off to a party, then on to dinner, after which Charlie asked, 'Your place or mine?' 'It was obvious that he really fancied me,' said Theresa. The inevitable bottle of champagne followed and then, as chat of team tactics tapered off, 'Charlie carried me into the bedroom. The difference between Charlie and other men is that he really cares about women and whether he's satisfying them . . . Charlie was an unbelievable lover. That night was pure magic. We talked about football but all he really wanted to talk about was sex . . . I can tell you, he certainly scored a hat-trick with me that night.'

All of this added much merriment to many a Sunday breakfast table and no doubt the chaps in the dressing room had a field day with Charlie. Theresa Bazar was one of a number of minor celebrity women Charlie had knocked around with during his time in London – as well as Suzanne Dando and Janis Lee Burns from the Flake advert, there'd also been topless model Linda Lusardi. What all these women had in common, apart from being important contributors to their various sporting and artistic fields, was the high frequency and indiscreet enthusiasm with which they submitted to the flash of the tabloid lightbulb.

Charlie loved glamour girls but he was often less keen than they were for photos of he and them whooping it up in Stringfellows or Tramps to be splashed across the papers. After all, Theresa Bazar and Suzanne Dando didn't have to face a carpeting from Don Howe the morning after their high jinks.

All of this, however, was a long time ago. And now, weeks after returning to Scotland, Charlie announced his engagement to Claire McKeown, who worked in the glitzy setting of a transport company near Stirling. Charlie had met Claire at a Celtic dance fully five years earlier before moving to Arsenal. Now he was back in Scotland and determined to settle down with the girl he left behind. The symbolism of all this was lost on nobody – Roving Prince Charlie leaves his sweet, homespun lass for the bright lights of London Town, but returns five years on, older, wiser and jilted, to bonny Scotland and his bonny lass. It was, on paper the stuff of revoltingly saccharine romantic ballads – but it was sweet and it was true.

Charlie was laying down roots in business, too, although here his fortunes weren't as universally happy. He'd bought a share in a Glasgow bar, Dexy's – but the roof had caved in and they'd been forced to shut the place for two months over the busy New Year. Another bar in which Charlie had a co-stake, the Nobody's Inn, off St. Enoch's Square, had run into trouble after a University newsletter took the bar to court over the matter of an unpaid bill of £379.80.

On the pitch at Aberdeen Charlie lined up alongside a team that included Jim Leighton, Willie Miller, Alex McLeish and Jim Bett. He didn't make an immediate impact – three goals in 15 games didn't auger well. He hadn't really gotten the Arsenal experience out of his system. His treatment at the hands of George Graham still rankled and he was still sufficiently recently out of London to be on call to journalists for good copy and jaundiced comment about Arsenal's still not entirely settled form.

If Charlie hadn't yet shaken off the ill-feelings surrounding his latter months at Arsenal, neither had he lost the surplus poundage that he'd acquired during that time. When it all went pear-shaped at Arsenal, so did Charlie. Emlyn Hughes's crack about the generosity of Charlie's derrière had had more than an ounce of truth about it. Simply put, Charlie wasn't match-fit. Some said that he'd boozed his way through the melancholy of rejection, a sure way of guaranteeing an expanded circumference. Whatever, when Scottish fans had been told they were going to see a lot more of Charlie, this wasn't quite what they'd had in mind.

At the beginning of the 1988-89 season, Ian Porterfield had given way as manager to Alex Smith. A fresh pair of eyes quickly spotted what the problem had been. 'Charlie was woefully unfit,' said Smith. 'He had to be taken care of – we had a frank exchange of views on the subject. He couldn't get away from defenders, and his attitude and confidence had suffered.'

To remedy the problem, Smith brought Operation Streamline Charlie into play. He sent Charlie to a sprint expert to sharpen up Charlie's capacity to accelerate – and to a boxing coach, who recommended half an hour's swimming every morning as a cure for the tiredness Charlie suffered in his much-buffeted hamstrings every time he ran.

The upshot of this was that Charlie shed a stone in a matter of weeks – he was in the best shape he'd been in for five years, surprising even himself. It dawned on Charlie now that one of the reasons for his lengthy bouts of sluggishness while at Arsenal had been down to their meat-and-potatoes training programme. He could kick himself now for not kicking up more of a fuss about it, and expounded at length on the subject in an interview with *The Times*.

'At Arsenal, it was all geared to coaching sessions. It slows the whole thing down. Suddenly your fitness becomes a problem if you don't look after it – which I didn't. Maybe I needed somebody to show me. Some players need to work on their ball skills. What I needed was just hard work but not the English kind.

'In Scotland we train far harder than the English boys. They can probably do more physically demanding things like cross country and think they're fit. But they don't do the hard work with the ball, although I know Liverpool do it. We were overcoached at Arsenal. That's why we struggled and looked an average team with so many good players.

'At Celtic, it was constant football, constant hard work. The hardest part of the game is being able to dribble, beat two or three men and still have the energy to finish.'

New Charlie extended his new spirit of contrition and frustration for what he increasingly referred to as his 'wasted' years at Arsenal to his parents. 'I accept that I sometimes broke my parents' hearts,' he told journalist Bryan Cooney. 'Nowadays I care a great deal about the reputation of my family but when you're young, you don't particularly care. I was blind to any problems while I was looked upon as a potential star. My folks were hurt very badly when people compared my off-the-field actions to those of George Best. It was debasing to see how they suffered in virtual silence. My father, especially, was very subdued. Normally, he's an extremely lively character like myself. He works in the newspaper industry in Glasgow and he had to go in there and experience people's cruel humour about me. He took it very badly.'

Charlie began to establish himself at Pittodrie, his natural, winning exuberance capturing the affections of everyone associ-ated with the club – he would bring in his sheepdog Jara to the ground, who would augment Charlie's singing in the bath after training with a barking, harmonic accompaniment that rang unmistakably around Pittodrie. The fans took to Charlie bigtime too, as, increasingly, unburdened of the physical and psycho-logical baggage of his Arsenal years, he notched up a brace of spectacular goals that put Aberdeen in a challenging position in the Premiership. By the end of January 1989, he was even back in the Scottish squad. 'He looks in international form,' said Scotland manager Andy Roxburgh.

Everything was going so well – until, in late February 1989, a bombshell fell. All that Charlie had worked for, all of his efforts to turn his life around were thrown, suddenly and appallingly, into jeopardy by two, terrifyingly ominous paragraphs in the *Daily Mirror*.

'SOCCER STAR FACES CHARGES', ran the headline. The offence was unspecified but hinted at a 'public nuisance', too dark and sordid to be reprinted in all its hideous, graphic detail in a family newspaper. Further details were as yet unavailable – but the procurator-fiscal was considering whether to prosecute and now Charlie's fate and reputation hung by a thread in the balance.

A few days later, the charge was read out. Urinating in public. Late at night, in an alleyway. £25 fine. Christ, was that all? The tabloids hadn't lost their sense of drama and magnification when it came to Charlie.

New Charlie was doing just fine at Aberdeen – but within days of joining the club it hadn't taken much prompting for him to confess aloud that, in his heart, he was still a Celtic fan. By March of 1989, rumblings and rumours that Celtic were looking to gather back their lost sheep into the Parkhead fold prompted the following outburst from manager Alex Smith.

'How often does Charlie have to say he is happy at Aberdeen to stop these rumours? It is absolute rubbish to suggest that Charlie is leaving or is anything less than happy here.

'Anyway, if Celtic were to make an offer it would anger me to think we couldn't resist it. We can afford to keep valuable assets. This whole thing is a complete fabrication.'

So there it was. There could be very little doubt about it. Charlie Nicholas was on his way back to Celtic.

Chapter Twelve

Actually 13 months would pass before Charlie finally made the move back to Parkhead. But it slowly became clear to Aberdonians that his twinkle-toed feet were getting increasingly itchy. He put in a transfer request in October 1989 and yet again kindled speculation that he might go to play on the continent, perhaps with Eintracht Frankfurt. Ironically, in creating for Charlie the fitness programme that had brought about his current spate of lithe prowess, Alex Smith had created a rod for his own back. Now that people were seriously talking about a revival of his international career in time for the 1990 World Cup, Charlie's newfound sense of self-belief conjured up dreams of new horizons beyond mere Pittodrie. (In the event, he didn't make the cut for Italia '90 – he had to content himself with sitting at home and watching Scotland crash out uselessly, duffed by Costa Rica in their opening game.)

That said, Charlie was still scoring goals, as assiduously against Celtic as anyone else. One, in a Premiership match in

February 1990 lit an inextinguishable memory in the minds of those who was it. Goalkeeper Mimms hoofed the ball upfield, Gilhaus headed the ball on – and Charlie, at an angle, swivelled and caught it crisp on the volley, sending it crashing into the back of the net. The ball never actually touched the ground – this was route one with a difference, route one with a rare flash of spontaneity, opportunism and panache. It was one of those Charlie Moments that, though you might sit through five or six games waiting for them to arrive, were such a delicious prospect that merely the thought that they might occur at any moment was pleasurable enough in itself.

Charlie himself, however, was notoriously ambivalent about scoring against Celtic. In a meeting with them at Parkhead, he slotted one home but showed no pleasure, or emotion of any kind. This angered sections of the Aberdeen support – Charlie was substituted. As he came off, Celtic fans saluted him and chanted his name.

His last game for Aberdeen would be the Scottish Cup Final of 1990 against Celtic. By this time, Billy McNeill had agreed terms and he knew he was on his way back. The first 90 minutes were a stale, deadlocked, goalless affair – extra time produced no more goals either as a tight, wary game lumbered inexorably towards the first-ever penalty shoot out in a Scottish Cup Final.

Charlie, needless to say, was one of the penalty takers. As he stepped up, he knew he would be a Celtic player within a matter of months. The fans would have known the same. And he knew that they knew. And they knew that he knew that they knew – anyway, such are the tortuous wrestlings of the mind in these situations. Sod it. He stepped up. He scored. He later said that his professional pride would never have let him fluff the shot. But never can a penalty goal in a Cup Final have been converted with so little enthusiasm.

Charlie was signed to Parkhead for £450,000. 'My heart has always been at Celtic,' he said. He would have been heartened to know he had appreciated in value in 18 months but some supporters weren't sure that he was such a wonderful buy, his lack of pace being a question mark. That McNeill had also paid £650,000 for Martin Hayes, whom George Graham had rated as 'just as big a star as Charlie Nicholas' made some fans wonder aloud if McNeill had taken leave of his marbles. Hayes was a disaster, playing only ten games before being released on a free transfer.

As for Charlie, he too had an indifferent and injury-hit season. He scored his first goal on returning to the club on December 15, against Hibernian – and then, with his customary Yuletide benevolence, knocked in a couple more in the run-up to Christmas Day, though unfortunately he was the only one – Celtic were on a losing streak. But by March he had only appeared in the starting line-up eight times.

He went into an April 5 fixture against Dunfermline an unhappy man, sensing that the way things were going, this could be his last game for the club. In the event, he had a stormer. As Celtic romped home 5-1, Charlie scored two himself, one a neat drag-back followed by a rifling left-foot drive, and set up two more for Tommy Coyne, with some deft interplay. Charlie was given a standing ovation as he left the pitch – fervent, if slightly histrionic Celtic watchers talked of the Second Coming.

Charlie scored twice more in the last three games as Celtic won their last four home matches – thereby qualifying at the last gasp for a UEFA Cup place, after a season that had been woeful in patches. It hadn't been enough to save McNeill's hide, however – the board had been meaning to sack him earlier in the season but Celtic kept winning key games just as they were about to make the announcement.

There had been talk of either Kenny Dalglish or Lou Macari taking over at the helm – Charlie would have baulked at the latter with his reputation for playing joyless, safety-first, rear-guard football. In the event, however, these names had been thrown out as decoys. The new manager, it was announced on June 19 1991, would be 35-year-old Liam Brady, taking up his first such post. A legend in British football, he had always seemed too ethereally brilliant for the English game and it had been no surprise, though a source of regret, when he eventually ascended from this rude earth to the celestial heights of Italian football. A delicate novice, he set out his stall at the outset – he wanted to play a 'skilful passing game, one where the people watching are going to be entertained'.

All of this was U2 to Charlie's ears. Though it was perhaps a surprise that given his declared philosophy, his first venture into the transfer marketplace saw him come back home carrying a large package in the form of Tony Cascarino, a tall, ungainly forward who might as well have been on stilts for all the intricacy he'd hitherto shown on the ball. Still, Charlie had played Jack and the Beanstalk before alongside Niall Quinn at Arsenal, and he settled in nicely behind Cascarino and Tommy Coyne that season. In spite of his role as a playmaker, he racked up 21 goals in the Premiership alone, his best total since his 1982-83 season at Celtic.

Charlie had complained more than once about the state of Scottish football since his return. It was similar to his complaint about English football. 'It's all about working. Players are asked to go out and chase and harry and co-ordinate pace and strength and aggression. If the skilful player in Scotland gets the ball he is closed down, pressurised and probably kicked.'

Under Liam Brady Charlie was the main beneficiary of a 'cultural revolution', in which, as one Scottish writer put it, passing, rather than passion was the order of the day. Nicholas contrasted the sharper training regimen he now enjoyed under Brady with the squarebashing, bulkbuilding nonsense he felt he'd had to endure at Arsenal. 'Every Monday morning at Arsenal the players were in the gym lifting massive weights to build up bulk – I put on pounds but lost speed and mobility. At Parkhead, we only use light weights to increase muscle tone – not size or weight. Liam Brady's experience in Italy has taught him how to get the best out of players physically, and in my case he obviously tries to protect me a wee bit,' said Charlie.

Unfortunately, while Charlie was enjoying himself, the team as a whole were under a siege of criticism. For one thing, while they were seeing off the relative crofters of Dunfermline and the like easily enough, they were regularly coming off worst in the Old Firm clashes. Ever since David Murray's cash injection and the arrival of Graeme Souness as manager, Rangers had enjoyed a runaway dominance in the Scottish Premiership which to this day has yet to be overhauled. Celtic were being made to look smaller and smaller. It was all very well the team playing pretty, ornamental football, but they weren't winning the big games and supporters were getting hacked off.

This was shown in their lukewarm response to Celtic's opening round home victory over Belgians Germinal Ekeren, which Celtic won 2-0, thanks to two Charlie Nicholas goals, including one penalty. Yeah, fine, good result, but Christ, if Celtic couldn't beat a team with a name like that, there was very little point in bothering.

Come the next round and Celtic were up against mighty Swiss foes in the form of Neuchatel Xamax. Away from home, the Bhoys put in the worst performance they'd ever registered in Europe, one which would have made the Lisbon Lions put their paws to their eyes in despair – they lost 5-1. Even so, Neuchatel Xamax had looked so ordinary, there was hope that back at Parkhead a restoration to sanity could be achieved. This looked all the more on when Celtic were awarded a penalty in the opening minutes. Charlie, as ever stepped up. Uncommonly, however, his spot-kick acumen and sense of the key moment deserted him – he missed, a miss which pulled the plug on any hopes of a Celtic recovery.

Celtic won 1-0 on the night but the aggregate result was considered a disaster. Celtic hadn't just lost, hadn't just lost by a wide margin, but had lost to a team whose name had two Xs in it and was palindromic to boot. Somehow, that seemed to rub it in. Celtic fans today have surprisingly vague memories of the 20-odd goals Charlie did manage to convert that season. The memory of that penalty miss, however, lingers on. If it had been anyone else but Charlie, they'd have been barracked out of Parkhead. It didn't help any when Celtic were dumped out of the Scottish Cup by Rangers, 1-0 at Hampden Park. Having already been put out by Airdrieonians 4-2 on penalties in the Skol Cup, there were now no trophies to play for. Apathy set in on the terraces – attendances dropped to below the 15,000 level.

Off the field, meanwhile, Charlie was having his own problems, with reports that Café Cini, a bar in central Glasgow which he co-owned, was in debt to the tune of £142,000. The new season would being still less cheer. Liam Brady, who from the start of his managership had shown a shellshocked and unsteady hand in trying to cope with the various forces and pressures that came with management of an Old Firm team, tried to throw a bit of money at Celtic's predicament. As well as an Albanian defender, Vata, and Andy Payton from Middlesborough, he bought his young mate Stewart Slater from West Ham for £1.5 million, in what at the time must have looked a shrewd signing – small, speedy and skilful, Slater had been a quickfire dynamo at West Ham and just the sort of player Brady was looking for at Celtic, a younger version of the great man himself – but, like Brady, he didn't seem to be able to make any sort of dent at all at Parkhead.

Charlie Nicholas was lost in the reshuffle and lost his place in the team, reduced to helping out the kids in the reserves. He was bewildered and not a little hurt at his deselection – though he admitted that, at 30, he was unable to play a full 90 minutes any more, as his much-harassed ligaments weren't up to it. By March 1993, Charlie was the forgotten man of Parkhead. He'd made just one appearance as a substitute all season. When his recall was announced over the tannoy system, however, the response from the crowd wasn't 'Charlie Whocolas?' but the sort of rapturous cheer that greets the news that a big pop band of yesteryear is to reform.

In spite of Brady's signings and attempts to rebuild his backroom team, 1992/93 was to prove no more successful than the previous season. They were third in the Premiership once more, by Celtic standards an utter failure. They had meekly waved the white flag to Aberdeen in a 1-0 defeat in the Skol Cup Final – but far worse was to come, in a prototype of the disaster that would eventually unseat Tommy Burns. Celtic travelled up to Brockville Park, came, saw and were conquered by Falkirk 2-0. A year earlier, after Celtic had lost to Airdrie, Brady had attempted to explain that, given that the latter were a tough, physical, fellow-Premiership side, there was no shame in the defeat. Someone had mumbled then, 'Liam, Celtic just doesn't lose to teams like Airdrie.' If defeat to Airdrie was unthinkable, defeat to Falkirk was unforgivable. Brady wasn't actually out the door yet, but the directors were, so to speak, suggesting coffee and dropping hints about excellent mini-cab firms.

At the beginning of the 1993/94 season, Brady was still hanging in there but both he and his team seemed too fragile to withstand the continuing slings and arrows of outrageous home defeats. He'd been forced to sell his beloved Stuart Slater at half

what he'd paid for him – some said, to placate the Bank of
Scotland and the wolf that was clawing at the Celtic door. In
October, after defeat at St Johnstone, Liam Brady decided to
jump before he was pushed.

His replacement would be, to Charlie Nicholas's quiet
chagrin, Lou Macari, whose attitude to how the game should be
played was directly antithetical to Charlie's – workrate, discipline, route one. But he'd actually been chosen by the Celtic
board less for his footballing philosophy than his reputation for
being able to get decent results on a shoestring budget – which,
the Lord knew, Celtic were on right now. For Parkhead was in the
grip of a financial and administrative crisis which would turn the
club inside out, provoke rebellion and civil war and see ancient
dynasties toppled – and Charlie came out on the winning side.

At the root of the problem was parsimony. The Celtic board had
been dominated, since their early days, by three families: the
Whites, the Grants and the Kellys. Celtic's first captain had been
one James Kelly, who served as chairman and when he died in
1932 was succeeded as director by his son Bob. So it went on
with the families, down the line even into the nineties. Critics of
the set-up, compared their running of the club to that of a corner
shop. There was a widespread feeling that the board hadn't actually wanted Celtic to win the European Cup in 1967 because of
the onus this placed on them to expand, think big, modernise –
Lord forbid, even inject some capital into the club! This,
however, they stoutly refused to do. The Lisbon Lions had
always been loyal – but thereafter, whenever great players rose

through the Celtic ranks, the board refused to match the sort of offers they were liable to get from the big English clubs, and off they went. That's what happened to Kenny Dalglish, and that's what happened to Charlie Nicholas, who during his first phase at Celtic was on something like £280 a week plus an £80 goal bonus. Billy McNeill had left too after he realised that, although Celtic team were dominant team in Scotland at that point, he was on far lower wages than his opposite numbers at Rangers, Aberdeen and Dundee United. Even in 1967 he had only been on £60 a week.

Charlie had decided to go to London after an offer from the board that was practically an insult. When word was conveyed to the Celtic Chairman, Desmond White, that Charlie didn't intend to renew his contract, White's response consisted of one word: 'Good.'

The season after Charlie left, attendances dropped dramatically, an implicit reproach to the club for having let Charlie go. In April of 1983, for instance, 34,508 fans watched Celtic beat Dundee United at home. In April of 1984, Celtic repeated their victory against the same team in front of just 4,956 fans. It amounted to an unofficial, perhaps unconscious boycott, a tactic that was to be used to much more concerted effort in the revolt of the nineties.

The board saw Celtic as a 'family club'. Dissenting elements in the press accused them of being more like feudal barons. 'Venal, self-serving and unambitious' were the kindest words one Scottish sports journalist could think of to describe them to me recently. Discontent was bad enough even when Celtic were winning the Premiership regularly. However, when Rangers shook themselves out of their own parochial crisis with the introduction of David Murray and his lolly in the mid-eighties, resentment began to boil over. And when the 'Gers poached former Celt Mo Johnston from under Celtic's noses from Nantes for £1.5 million, it was practically the end. It wasn't just sectarian bitterness at Mo's defection that galled – it was frustration that Celtic could not, would not have ever pulled off such an imaginative coup.

In May 1990, salvation of sorts seemed to have arrived in the form of Brian Dempsey, son of a Labour MP, a property developer and entrepreneur. He had been brought on board so that they might present a front of go-ahead modernism to the world. But when Dempsey outlined proposals for a new stadium to be built in the north-east area of the city, fellow directors clutched nervously at their wallets. Although Celtic's own stadium was a patched-up crumbling heap and still lagging behind the recommendations of the Taylor Report introduced after Hillsbrough, the very idea of a new stadium seemed to strike at the heart of all that they held in their bank accounts. Here was the problem – Celtic were a business with a multi-million pound turnover with minuscule capital. The dynasties that ran Celtic saw it as their birthright, with no concomitant responsibility.

In fact, one or two directors suspected that Dempsey didn't have the money to match his mouth and that, being in the property trade himself he was guilty of a conflict of interest – and they might have been able to make a decent case to this effect. However, in their handling of the situation, they showed an arrogance, high-handedness and insensitivity that would prove the final straw. At the club's Annual General Meeting in October, board members Michael Kelly and Chris White opposed Dempsey's ratification as director. And, though they were out-numbered, they had pooled together sufficient share power to make their vote decisive.

Dempsey's removal from the board was publicly announced on the eve of Celtic's meeting with Rangers in the Skol Cup Final. White and Kelly refused to be drawn on the reasons for their decision. It was in the midst of this club turmoil that Celtic players would go out for the Old Firm clash. It was hardly ideal preparation. Celtic lost.

Discontent would continue to ferment for two or three years, with attendances dwindling and fanzines such as *Not the View* providing a weekly barrage of sniper fire against the board. Dempsey was banished but not gone – he still had friends at the club, including Charlie Nicholas, who himself had interests in the building trade. McNeill left, Liam Brady came and went. And now, as Lou Macari stepped into the breach, the crisis was coming to a head, with the coffers emptying and pressure being brought to bear by the 'rebels', a group of disaffected supporters led by financial consultant David Low. He it was who had first undermined the board's shareholding power by pooling together the anger and resources of the many small, disgruntled shareholders. The board were further softened up by the announcement of their debts, some £5 million – that, plus the bill they'd eventually get for updating their ramshackle stadium.

The supporters played their part, too. Angered by a series of terrible results which reflected the parlous state of Celtic affairs, they held spontaneous 'Sack The Board!' demos outside the ground. During one disastrous 0-3 reversal against Rangers, one supporter is said to have turned away from the pitch towards the director's box, tied a knot in his scarf, noose-like and dangled it mercilessly at the board members in a tick-tock style for the remainder of the game. Time was running out.

Charlie sensed which way the wind was blowing. The players would have been expected to have kept out of all this but at this late stage of his career, he was his own man, more assertive, more outspoken, a man of more independent means than the wee young Mr Anything-To-Oblige he'd been in his early years. By late 1993, he began coming out in a series of interviews with the Scottish press and BBC Scotland. He was the first to break his silence and side openly with the rebels, who were now led by his friend, Brian Dempsey, from exile – and Fergus McCann. McCann was a Canadian-Scot and ardent Celtic fan who had made his fortune in the leisure industry stateside. He'd first offered his services to the club in 1988 but the board had seen him and his money off with a 'Not today, thank you'.

Now Fergus McCann was back for the kill. As 1993 turned into 1994, the tide was turning in the favour of the rebels. Demos continued outside the ground. Nicholas continued to speak his mind – as did captain Paul McStay and Pat Bonner among others. They came under great pressure from the management to keep their heads down, their mouths shut – but that wasn't Charlie's way any more. Hell, he was in continued litigation with Celtic in any case, a dispute over his initial signing-on fee. As for new boss Lou Macari, he didn't mind upsetting him. Lou had ushered in an era of hoof-and-hope football to Parkhead which to Charlie, who by now had no legs to be chasing about pointlessly upfield, was anathema – although he was in the team and scoring. Charlie continued to speak his mind. The old board, the people who were running the club were running the club down. It was time for them to go.

By now hopelessly divided, besieged and looking at a mountain of debt, the board in February 1994 desperately resuscitated the 'Cambuslang Dream' scheme, a £100 million superstadium to be built on a new site. They'd first announced the scheme in 1992, oblivious to the irony that it was for proposing just such a scheme that they had got rid of rebel Brian Dempsey. The board announced that the club would be floated on the stock exchange to raise the necessary share capital. Lou Macari, as manager and establishment man, gave the proposals such as they were, his public endorsement, saying they were a step in the right direction. In the same day, in the same paper, the *Glasgow Evening Herald*, Charlie Nicholas expressed his scepticism. 'I wonder if it's another delaying tactic,' he remarked, adding meaningfully, 'the reaction of our fans at the next game, in the light of talks of boycotts, will be very intriguing to me. The most important thing is how the supporters react.' As for the board, Charlie had only this to say, 'I know that at the end of my career I will come back and pay my way in to watch Celtic. They won't.'

No one seriously believed that this grocer-shop board, in the dotage of their influence, would really be able to pull off this sort of project. It was like watching the demented King Lear on the blasted heath ranting about his future plans and grand schemes. The board had said the scheme would be underwritten by a Swiss bank, Gefinor – but when someone contacted Gefinor in Geneva, its director said they didn't know what the hell they were talking about. No formal agreement had been signed at all. Contempt, scorn and derision were thus heaped on the board. 87 per cent of fans in a poll, agreed with Charlie – it was time for these people to go.

A boycott was arranged for the March 1 match against Kilmarnock. The official attendance was given as 10,882. Sceptical observers reckoned it was more like 7,000. Whatever, it was the death knell. The Bank of Scotland was now leaning on directors to underwrite the club's swelling debt as Celtic inched towards receivership. At the death, the McCann-Dempsey consortium beat off a rival bid to take over the club and provide the necessary cash injection. With the club literally minutes away from its receivership deadline, Fergus McCann flew in, did the paperwork and handed over a £5 million cheque as collateral. The rebels had won.

Charlie greeted the news with undisguised glee. 'This can be the start of a great new dawn for the club,' he declared, praising Brian Dempsey as a 'true Celt'. 'Now it's up to all of us to show they did the right thing in backing us.'

A very bitter outgoing Michael Kelly left with a settlement of £170,000 and a parting word of advice to Lou Macari – get rid of Charlie Nicholas.

Chapter Thirteen

Lou Macari did as Michael Kelly suggested. Nicholas was among five players who were informed their services were no longer required. The others were Frank McAvennie, Gary Gillespie, Pat Bonner and Wdowcyzk, a player the fans had always found hard to celebrate in rhyming song. Charlie had been issued a free transfer. Yet before the death warrant could be issued, Macari himself was ousted by Fergus McCann under circumstances which are still today the subject of pending litigation between the two parties.

Tommy Burns took over and retained Charlie – more for the sake of auld lang syne than anything else, really. He issued one caveat – that Charlie keep his nose out of club politics.

Charlie realised that he would never be able to keep pace with the young 'uns and his role was increasingly an avuncular, coaching one. It was in this capacity in March 1995 that he found himself at the centre of one of the saddest and unexpected episodes of his life.

Charlie had never allowed the intensity of his rivalry with Rangers to take the form of personal enmity between himself and anyone associated with the club. Many 'Gers fans loved Charlie. Jock Wallace, former Rangers manager had taken the trouble to devise for Charlie an exercise and diet programme during his second sojourn at Celtic. And Charlie numbered among his friends Rangers players, including winger Davie Cooper, with whom he participated in a televised coaching session in March 1995.

They'd just finished a set-piece and were jokingly rehearsing Charlie's introduction for the next scene. Unable to come up with a satisfactory wording, Charlie suggested they break off for a pint. A second later, and without any prior hint of distress, Davie collapsed. Charlie rushed off to call an ambulance but there was nothing to be done. Two days later, Davie Cooper had died, the tragic victim of a brain haemorrhage.

Charlie had one more big game in him for Celtic – the 1994-95 Scottish League Cup Final against modest Raith Rovers. It would have made a good testimonial for Charlie, a lovely last hurrah and looked like so being as he poked the ball in off a rebound to score what for all the world ought to have been the winning goal to put Celtic 2-1 up, with just six minutes to go. But after everything he'd done, all that he'd been through, Fate wouldn't allow Charlie a lovely, bow-tied ending to his career. Raith equalised with three minutes to go, the match went to extra time and Charlie's final curtain went unnoticed as all the talk was of plucky little Raith's 6-5 victory on penalties.

In July 1995, Charlie decided to leave Celtic for regular and less arduous footballing duties at Clyde. Alex Smith, formerly his manager at Aberdeen had enticed him there and Charlie looked forward to rounding off his career with some non-demanding exhibition football.

Some saw the move as a mistake. 'He was leagues above the rest of the players, it was ridiculous,' said one former colleague. What's more, he was the victim of every young upstart clogger coming up through the ranks of mediocrity who could proudly declare, I did that Charlie Nicholas, me.

For sure, Charlie was no spring chicken no more. He'd even taken to wearing a vest beneath his shirt. 'It's his age,' explained the backroom laundry lady.

But even this late on there were moments of sheer sorcery wasted on the desert air of Broadwood. One Clyde team-mate remembers being some 50 yards upfield and being delivered by the great man a perfectly weighted, perfectly flighted pass that landed plum like a pudding within inches of his feet – the most perfect pass he had ever received. Indeed, so in awe was he that he pushed the ball a hopeless 10 yards on with his first touch, to his eternal shame and embarrassment.

Then there was that Cup Tie in February 1996, when Charlie and Clyde had led Rangers 1-0 at home, and Charlie had the delicious, immortal temerity to nutmeg Paul Gascoigne on national TV. Even Gazza had to laugh.

Finally, after considering and then discarding an offer to play out in the Far East, Charlie hung up his boots for the last time. He was secure enough now – the Café Cini, once in jeopardy had turned the corner and is still open today. He has a family now –

two daughters, Nadine and Sophie – and a career lined up and ready-made for him – that of TV punditry. He'd been gabbing to and taking gab from the media for so many years that there was little he needed to learn. He straightaway picked up work at the Scottish *Daily Express*, Sky, STV and BBC Scotland, an able and articulate punter. Certain Celtic fans reckon he's turned traitor, believing he's over-generous in his tributes towards Rangers players such as Laudrup. And one or two were genuinely left cold when he seemed a little over-supportive towards Paul Gascoigne after the wife-beating incident. But then, examine his observations closer and more charitably and maybe he was empathizing with a creature similar to himself, a lost, uprooted soul, prone to temptations and frustrations.

As for Charlie's own past, well, the past is another country.

In many ways, Charlie Nicholas was a player ahead of his time. He was one of the first players to flaunt an agent. To celebrate goals with a customised dance routine. To enthuse about music a little more modern and adventurous than the usual chicken-in-a-basket MOR of Tina Turner and Rod Stewart generally favoured by footballers. To brave the guffaws of the locker room and take a serious interest in fashion. To shag celebrity ladies. All of this is mandatory in the modern game – Blur, Armani, Dani Behr. In Charlie's day, there were no role models or contemporaries to show him the way. He found his way alone, guided only by the compass of his irrepressible desire for a good crack.

On the field, he was among the first players to decry the joyless, high ball, defensive, mediocre muscularity of the modern game. Especially after his experiences at Arsenal, he was highly critical of the over-emphasis on tight defence, work rate, tracking back and harrying across every inch of the turf that had become the governing obsessions of the eighties game. It wasn't just players like himself that found themselves marginalised in the English First Division. Glenn Hoddle and Chris Waddle had been forced to take their wares abroad, prophets not without honour, save in their own country. In France it was a source of amazement that two players of their calibre couldn't command places in the England team.

Charlie complained volubly about the training regimen at Highbury, which had placed more emphasis on strength and stamina than on skill and technique. Later on, he revealed how throughout his years there he had been forced to take cortisone injections to block the pain in his ligaments, constantly harassed and chipped at by the sort of 'dogged', 'wholehearted', 'committed' defenders the game seemed to value above his own sort.

Although Charlie was a man of his times, he came up time and again against managerial men whose values seemed to belong in a bygone era of crewcuts, correct appearance and team effort. Jock Stein. George Graham. And yet, hidebound as the attitudes of these men might have been in the matter of earrings, the hard fact to face was that they were winners. George Graham, especially, could feel thoroughly vindicated by the record of the post-Nicholas Arsenal, who went on to win two championships, the FA Cup and the European Cup Winners' Cup under his stewardship. And dear God, didn't Arsenal fans appreciate that?

For the truth is that while Charlie Nicholas was ahead of his

time in all of these ways, while his analysis of the game prefigured some of the continental input we take for granted in
today's Premiership, he was also one of the last remaining
specimens of a bygone era. His jiggling, bamboozling style, the
way he took on defenders more out of delight in the tease rather
than the end result, were reminiscent of old-fashioned wingers
of bygone days, the Matthews, the Johnstones. Foreplay was
always as important to Charlie as bulging the back of the net. But
in the wingless, joyless, rush and bustle of the modern game
there is less and less time for such frippery. In the course of
researching this book I asked several people if maybe Charlie
might have thrived at Arsenal under the sympathetic tutelage of
an Arsene Wenger. Some politely suggested maybe so, others
reluctantly shook their heads. Trouble is, Charlie always lacked
pace – he'd have never caught up with the ultra modern game.
What's more, physical resilience was never quite his strong suit.
He was never quite quick or strong enough to evade the worst,
carnivorous attentions of brutal defenders. Jock Stein once
described Charlie as like a 'delicate piece of bone china',
summing up his beauty and fragility.

Charlie, of course, never fulfilled his potential. For some
people that is the end of the story. Like Orson Welles, his greatest successes were earliest on in his career. That's largely because
it was only then that he had sufficient 'legs' to make the most of
his quickthinking, slickjinking talents. At that point, reckoned
Tommy Burns, Charlie was 'the most talented young player in
Europe'. By his mid-twenties, he could only show in spurts.

Why, then, did he generate, then as now, such love among

fans? And such unconditional love at that? Danny Crainie recalls stopping over in London to watch Charlie in a cup game against Millwall, 'It was the worst game I'd ever seen him play, an absolute stinker. And yet the North Bank was cheering him throughout the entire game, 'Char-lee! Charlee!' I couldn't believe it!'

For Nick Hornby, it was the sense that with Charlie there was always 'the sense of potential. A bit like with Paul Merson these days. Even if he did something special four or five times a season it was always worth waiting for. And it was something you were never going to get with a Paul Mariner.'

For journalist Phil Gordon, Charlie, in his little war-dances, in his delightful fits and starts, was someone who 'translated the joy of playing football to the people watching. Nicholas was the fan who was out there playing and he didn't forget where he came from.'

Charlie fan and fanzine contributor James Payne speaks for many when he sees Charlie as a talent who simply headed in the wrong direction at the turnpike. 'He was the best player I've seen since Jimmy Johnstone and a far better player than Dalglish at the age of 21. The difference was that Dalglish went on to have a very full career and Charlie just had great moments. He should have stayed at Celtic – if he'd had real intelligence, he would have. Celtic were a better team than Arsenal at that time and he could really have developed. Then, two years down from the line, he wouldn't just have been looking at Arsenal, Liverpool and Man Utd. The Italians and the Spanish would have been fighting over him as well.

'For someone of his ability only to have own 20 caps seems ridiculous. It annoys me that Ally McCoist is probably the most successful Scottish player of the last ten years and he hasn't a tenth of Charlie's talent.'

Yet it might be that with players like Charlie, consistently and dependability was never quite the point. Top-class consistent and dependable players are a godsend to managers, but to what extent do they please the punters? Take Matt Le Tissier and Teddy Sheringham. You'd have to agree on the face of the facts as they stand that Teddy Sheringham ought to be in the England team above Matt Le Tissier. You'd agree. Teddy delivers, Matt doesn't. Yet who would choose a *Best of Teddy Sheringham* video over a *Best of Matt Le Tissier*? And while a well-taken Teddy Sheringham goal against a Georgia or a Poland is good, can you imagine the joy, the dancing, the laughter and elation if Matt Le Tissier were at last to lumber along and drive in one of his long-rangers out of nothing for England? Dependability we've got already.

Denis Law, when asked if Charlie Nicholas was as good as Dalglish, once snapped, 'When Charlie has played 100 games for Scotland and scored 30 goals then I'll be able to give you an answer. Until then, it's a pretty stupid question.'

Former colleague Frank McGarvey was nearer to the point. 'If Charlie had only scored 20 goals in that season for Celtic instead of 51, the fans would still have loved him.'

Managers see football as a matter of winning at all costs and by whatever means, within the rules, or – mostly within the rules. Great victories, cup triumphs, league success, all of these things are rare enough to be worth battling tooth and nail until every capilliary bursts on your face. Yet what Charlie offered was even rarer. Cheek, style, a twinkle here, a starburst there. Even opposition fans used to get it. Sometimes, if he was setting himself up for a corner or even jogging up and down the touch-line, fans would give him grief – and he'd start preening his hair, in some parody of the great big poof their moronic element liked to take him for. The desperation, the hustle and bustle, the frantic, win-at-all costs spirit, the dog-eat-dog brutality, the squeezing out of leisure and joy in the headlong rush to 'get things done' – all of these are things with the modern game but you could just as easily be talking about modern life. Charlie railed against that. His spontaneity, his sense of fun – when he took on defenders, it was almost as if he was taking on the brute, tedious forces of churlish reality. And, of course, reality had its way on Charlie in the end, especially on his hacked ligaments. But Charlie on song was an inevitably fleeting throwback to a merrier, Arcadian age.

So what, then, if Charlie never achieved his potential? So what if Charlie didn't cover every inch of the turf, score as many goals as he could have, run his heart out the way he might have done? There are more important things. If Charlie couldn't quite find a role in the game to flourish in then you could almost feel that that was the fault of the game, not Charlie. He might have said of himself, after former screen star Gloria Swanson in *Sunset Boulevard*, 'I was always big. It was the pitches that got small.'

Why else was Charlie loved? Well, after Smashie and Nicey it's impossible to commend anyone for their charidee work with a straight face, and after Tim Nice-But-Dim it's still harder to call anyone a 'Bloody nice bloke'. But . . . let's have a go.

Charlie never refused autographs. He'd once tried to ask Kenny Dalglish for his and had been paralysed by cold feet. Though he loved being a star, he never wanted anyone to feel like that in his presence.

Says Tom Watt, 'I don't think fans were particularly interested in all that Champagne Charlie stuff. It didn't make them like him any more or any less. It was just sort of tolerated. But I've an awful lot of time for the man, for the stuff he did that never got any publicity. I'm sure he had a good time on a Saturday night. But what was rare among players was him turning up on a Sunday morning for the charity games, no matter how ropey he was feeling. I know, from things I was involved in. He was a good feller and an honourable feller. And . . . he was just that bit short of pace!'

John Colquhoun remembers one game Charlie played for Aberdeen. It was a Scottish Cup game at Pittodrie and Charlie wasn't having a good game. In fact, the crowd were beginning to get a bit exasperated. Then, with seven minutes to go, he finally scored – and the first thing he did was rush over to a little child, about five years old, who'd been sitting on the wall at the front of the terraces getting soaked – and held him aloft in triumph. He said he'd promised himself he'd give the lad a hug if he scored because through all the rain and barracking all he could hear was this boy shouting 'Char-LEE! Char-LEE!'

Everybody's favourite. In the summer of 1991, Paul Davis was given his testimonial match by Arsenal. They'd play Celtic.

Chapter Thirteen

Mindful of the lousy reception Charlie had received when he returned to Parkhead, Charlie was apprehensive. He'd never had his chance to say goodbye to the fans at Highbury. He hoped no ill-will had been harboured. After all, he'd had a go at the club, he'd said maybe he should have joined Liverpool.

Charlie turned it on. Playing behind Coyne and Cascarino he was pulling all the strings. Highbury warmed and warmed. After one lovely move, a wave of applause. Charlie took a bow. Then he took up the ball 35 yards out, nutmegged Limpar which got a laugh – and crashed it against the bar. At the end, buoyed up by an intense jumble of emotions, Charlie ran to the North Bank, tore off his Celtic shirt and hurled it triumphantly into the crowd, to an ecstatic ovation, a very warm, very poignant, very forever, very Charlie moment.

Moments like that are rarer than double-winning seasons.

One final reason to love Charlie. His panache, yes. His teasing dribbles, yes. His sense of fun and occasion, yes. He was, indeed, the classic and veritable pop footballer. But there is something for which we should be still more thankful. Something that ranks him apart from some of our finest footballing superstars, Glen Hoddle, Chris Waddle, Kevin Keegan, even Gazza. Great as the temptation was, he never made a pop record.

Cheers, Charlie.

Further titles in the goal series . . .

Mickey Thomas: Wild at Heart

Mickey Thomas is a living legend, but not for his uncanny knack of scoring spectacular goals during his time at Manchester United, Chelsea and Wrexham, nor for his fifty-one caps for Wales.

Thomas is best remembered for serving time for laundering counterfeit ten-pound notes, and for being stabbed with a screwdriver when caught in a car, *in flagrante* with a married woman.

WALK-OUTS, BUST-UPS, WOMEN AND DRINK, WITH SOME INSPIRED FOOTBALL ALONG THE WAY, MICKEY THOMAS'S ROLLER-COASTER CAREER ON AND OFF THE PITCH IS A STORY THAT DESERVES TO BE TOLD

Kevin Keegan: Reluctant Messiah

Kevin Keegan's playing career was a triumph of will over skill. Nurtured by the great Bill Shankly, at his peak he ranked amongst the greatest in the world. Called out of retirement to manage the club he had saved as a player, he pulled Newcastle United from the brink of Second Division relegation to within reach of Premiership victory.

Yet trophies eluded him and as the pressures mounted, his controversial decisions and passionate involvement in the game attracted more attention than the football his team was playing.

KEEGAN'S MID-SEASON RESIGNATION SHOCKED THE COUNTRY. HOW HAD THE MESSIAH OF TYNESIDE FALLEN FROM GRACE?

Order Form

Please send me:

❑ 07522 2481 6   **MICKEY THOMAS:**
                            Wild at Heart   5.99
                            by Andy Strickland

❑ 075222476 X   **KEVIN KEEGAN:**
                            Reluctant Messiah   5.99
                            by Michael Hodges

TO: **Macmillan Distribution Ltd.,** Direct Customer Services,
      Brunel Road, Houndmills, Basingstoke, Hants RG21 6XZ
TEL: 01256 302 699
FAX: 01256 364 733

HOW TO PAY

Please charge my Access/Visa/Amex/Diners Club for £ _____

Account Number _____

Expiry Date _____

I enclose a cheque for £ _____ payable to Macmillan

Distribution Ltd.

Name _____

Address _____

_____

Postcode_____

Signature _____ Telephone _____

FREE POSTAGE AND PACKING!
in UK and Eire only
Please allow 28 days for delivery.
Price and availability subject to change without notice.